S0-AKT-310

MICHELANGELO

C

ONTENTS

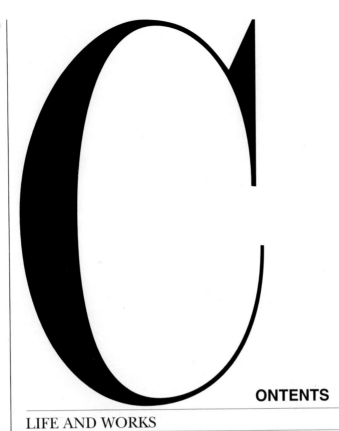

**Cover:
Michelangelo,
study for Porta Pia.
Florence,
Casa Buonarroti.**

**Right:
capital.
Florence,
Casa Buonarroti.**

Life and works
Bruno Contardi

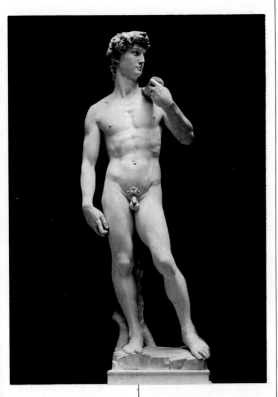

David (1501-1504).
Florence,
Galleria
dell'Accademia.

Symbolizing the virtues of the young Florentine Republic, the statue was intended to stand proudly alone at the entrance to Palazzo della Signoria.

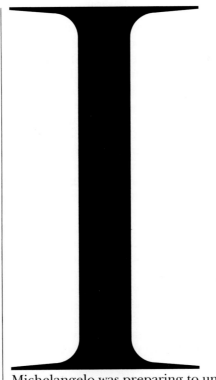

N APRIL 1508, WHEN Michelangelo was preparing to undertake the immense, as well as physically demanding task of painting the ceiling of the Sistine chapel, he was thirty-three years old. 'Enfant prodige' of Florentine culture and favoured by Lorenzo il Magnifico who had invited him to Palazzo Medici, his education was greatly influenced by the Neoplatonic philosophy of that society. From an early age, therefore, he had frequented the most learned Humanists of the day including the poet, Poliziano, the philosopher, Marsilio Ficino and the celebrated scholar, Pico della Mirandola. He joined Ghirlandaio's workshop and attended Bertoldo's school. However his education was more influenced by the examples of the great Florentine artists of the early 15th century, identifying more readily with Masaccio, Donatello, Jacopo della Quercia, and going even further back to the contemporaries of Dante such as Giotto and Nicola and Giovanni Pisano. Encouraged to study the vast Medici collection of antiquities, he gained his knowledge of classical art directly from original statues.

Before he was twenty years old he had sculpted the *Battle of Hercules and the Centaurs,* now in Casa Buonarroti, probably at the suggestion of Poliziano; at the age of twenty-two he had already gained fame in Rome where he had sculpted the *Pietà* now in Saint Peter's, possibly as a funerary monument for the ambassador of Charles VIII. In 1501 he was commissioned to make the enormous statue of *David* for Piazza della Signoria; in 1504, competing with the elderly Leonardo, he prepared the cartoon for the fresco of the *Battle of Cascina* in the Great Council Hall in Palazzo Vecchio.

In these key works Michelangelo had already tackled and redefined some of the most basic concerns of Florentine society at the end of the 15th century. The classical theme of *Hercules and the Centaurs* is not, as in Bertoldo's work, an excuse for a sophisticated formal exercise, nor, as for Piero di Cosimo, an elegiac, almost nostalgic evocation of a forgotten past, nor is it the inspiration for an imaginative composition of bizarre motifs, as in Filippino Lippi. For Michelangelo history is, in fact, the consequence of divine intervention in the world, and the antique is concrete evidence of this. The frantic fray represents the struggle between divinity and bestiality, the contrast between pure, unstructured, or barely formed material and the fury which 'transforms' itself into (or rather, assumes the form of) movement.

Movement is not, therefore, as Leonardo believed at the time, a phenomenon whose physical and mechanical causes can be studied, nor the result of recognizable anatomical forces, as in Pollaiolo's contemporary sculptures: for Michelangelo it is the materialization of divine inspiration which transcends all. In contrast to the eruption of cyclonic confusion in the *Battle of Hercules and the Centaurs*, an unearthly stillness transcends the marble *Pietà* in Saint Peter's; here Michelangelo confronted the problem of religion which tormented Botticelli and beset Signorelli during this period of bitter religious ferment (in May 1498, the Dominican priest, Girolamo Savonarola was burnt at the stake in Florence, tragically ending an experience which was not only religious in its implications). There is a simple explanation for the complete absence of movement and effort seen in the *Pietà* (even Christ's arm slowly relaxes, its calculated languor forming part of the triangular composition): movement and effort must be absent since the sacred, in contrast to Botticelli's apocalyptic view, is superior to and not in conflict with history – it surpasses the physical and material. The apparent contradiction of the youth of the Virgin who, in a naturalistic image, would be portrayed considerably older at the time of the death of the Son, has frequently been commented on. The sacred, however, does not conform to history as it exists neither in the past nor in the future, and its only possible temporal relationship is the absolute and contemporary immediacy of a 'vision', as indeed the *Pietà* must be considered. This also explains the absolute perfection of the marble, for all trace of the materialness of the sculpture must be eliminated and any sign of the technique concealed. Unhindered by sharp corners or edges the light flows over the highly polished surface creating an image which is more 'real' or vivid than in nature.

When he agreed to sculpt, for the Opera del Duomo of Florence, an immense *David* (more than four metres high) from a large block of marble which had already been rough-hewn forty years earlier by Agostino di Duccio, Michelangelo tackled the humanistic theme of the hero. During the 15th century sculptures

**The precise subject
of the relief
is uncertain though
it probably represents
divine intervention to
end the battle
between the Centaurs
and the Lapiths
after the abduction
of Hippodamia.**

Pietà
(1497-1498).
Rome,
church
of Saint Peter's,
Vatican.

were considered to be a celebration of man and his actions in history and in the world. Leon Battista Alberti propounded the theory in his work *De statua*, Donatello demonstrated it in his sculptures (such as the *Gattamelata* or the *Judith*) and Paolo Uccello and Andrea del Castagno in painting (one has only to think of the two equestrian monuments to Giovanni Acuto/John Hawkwood and Nicolò da Tolentino frescoed on the walls of Santa Maria del Fiore, or of the *Famous Men* originally in the villa at Legnaia to realise that we are dealing with a concept, rather than simply an artistic technique, as it is not confined to sculpture alone).

Compared to earlier statues however, Michelangelo's *David* is neither a triumphant hero flaunting the symbol of victory, nor a warrior seen in the struggle of battle: the huge figure is tense, concentrated, as taut as a spring accumulating tension to be released in a single movement which is latent in the statue. None of the action has yet occurred, the strength is not yet unleashed. The entire weight of the body rests on the right leg, the muscles of which are taut with strain, while the left is flexed forward creating a balanced asymmetry, continued in the left arm, bent to loosen the sling while the right is relaxed, except for the clenched hand. The greatest accumulation of energy is concentrated at the top of the statue in the muscles of the neck which give the head an aggressive, though controlled, twist. The expression of the face, too, is tense, the eyes fixed on the enemy still in the distance, the brows frowning. The very surface of the marble reveals an internal tension in the pulsing veins, tense muscles and prominent bones, demonstrating an anatomical expertise which is not evident in either the 'non-finito' of the *Centaurs* or the 'troppo-finito' of the *Pietà*. Even while in the making the deeper significance of the work altered, turning from a religious symbol into an essentially political statement: the immense nude was seen by Michelangelo himself as the incarnation of Fortitude and Ire, civic representations of the virtues of the people and the young Florentine Republic. The hero is therefore the symbolic representation of a concept, of an idea which becomes incarnate in history.

The only work signed by Michelangelo, in 1499 the statue was placed in the chapel of Saint Petronilla in Rome, where the French cardinal who commissioned the work, Jean Bilhères, was buried. In 1517 it was moved to the old sacristy in Saint Peter's. It has been in its present location since 1749.

Bastiano da Sangallo,
copy of the
Battle of Cascina.
Norfolk,
Holkham Hall,
Leicester collection.

As soon as the statue was finished, a public debate opened concerning the best location: probably Michelangelo, and most certainly the representative of the Signoria, wished to place it beside the entrance to Palazzo Vecchio, with the rough, old walls behind providing a contrast to the finely sculpted outline of the marble. Leonardo, instead, suggested it should be located in Orcagna's loggia "with a black niche behind, like a small chapel", thus giving it a chiaroscuro setting which would filter the shades and tones of the passing light and attenuate its absolute autonomy in relation to the surrounding space and atmosphere. Clearly this indicates a deep divergence between two opposing concepts which went far beyond ethics.

The difference of opinion became confrontation and then direct conflict when, the same year, Leonardo and Michelangelo were both commissioned by Pier Soderini to fresco the Great Council Hall in Palazzo Vecchio with scenes of two glorious battles in the history of the city: Leonardo was to represent the battle of Anghiari and Michelangelo the battle of Cascina. Neither work was ever finished however: Leonardo began work on the painting but the experimental technique he had decided to adopt was unsuccessful and the work was ruined; Michelangelo renounced the commission even before taking up his paintbrushes. While

Anonymous,
copy of the
Battle of Anghiari
by Leonardo
da Vinci,
(16th century).
Florence,
Galleria degli Uffizi.

Pitti Madonna (1503-1506). Florence, Bargello Museum.

they still remained intact, the preparatory cartoons were left on display and were enthusiastically studied by young Florentine artists. Cellini referred to them as "the school of the world" and for a long time they represented the most modern artistic statement in a city which was soon to be abandoned by its most famous sons, a definitive announcement of the end of the 15th century, and a spectacular start to the new century, dominated by Rome.

The theme this time was historical painting and the formal problem to resolve was how to co-ordinate and arrange so many figures in movement in a space which was unusual for the time (the wall to be frescoed was seven metres long).

A few copies of the *Battle of Anghiari* have survived and the oldest and closest to the original, now in Munich, most probably reproduces the only section actually to have been frescoed, the *Fight for the Standard*, later copied by Rubens among others. However, autograph sketches and studies of heads, horses,

The figure has no contextual space, but emerges from the surface with a powerful rotational movement.

9

knights and soldiers, have also survived and these provide a fairly clear idea of the artist's intention.

Even more interesting, however, is the passage which Leonardo wrote some years earlier on "how to portray a battle", where his advice was as follows, "You will first paint the smoke of the artillery, mingling in the air with the dust raised by the commotion of horses and combatants, and you will do it in this way: since dust is terrestrial and has weight, although its feminine fineness rises and mingles in the dusty air, it just as happily falls to the ground again and it is at its finest where it has risen highest: thus make it less visible there, so it looks almost like the air itself... show the victors charging, with their hair and other light things flying in the wind... show the vanquished and defeated pale, their eyebrows raised high ... Have all kinds of weapons lying underfoot: broken shields, lances, stumps of swords and other such things; have dead men, some partly covered with dust, others entirely covered and the dust mingling with the blood, turning it into red mud, and have red streams of blood running from the body into the dust; the dying will be grinding their teeth, rolling their eyes heavenwards, their fists clenched against their bodies and their limbs contorted". Smoke, blood, dust, cannon fire are all mingled in a cosmic, tumultuous maelstrom, amidst fierce expressions and suffering faces, the furious whinnying of horses excited by battle. For Leonardo the battle is akin to primordial chaos, a complete upheaval of nature, like an earthquake, a raging storm, exceptional events which Leonardo studied in many drawings during this period.

Exceptional, but nevertheless still part of the same laws of nature which control the orderly flow of things; and in battles, as in natural events, light, filtered by smoke and dust, alters forms and colours, just as rage and violence alter the expressions and appearance of the faces of men and animals, a caricature which modifies natural expressions and appearance.

While for Leonardo history is a natural event, for Michelangelo, as for Machiavelli in the *Discorsi*, it is power, will, the use of strength and energy. Instead of representing the battle in all its dreadful confusion, basing himself on Villani's *Chronica* he decided to portray an event before the victory, when Manno Donati raised the alarm, rousing the Florentine troops, who had paused to refresh themselves in the cool waters of the river after the long march towards Pisa. The cry "We're lost!", the fear of being attacked unprepared at the decisive moment has stirred the nude figures into action.

The copy of part of the preparatory cartoon made in the mid-16th century by Bastiano da Sangallo shows a composition consisting of a series of diverging triangles starting with the rocky banks of the riverside and extending into the background, as in a marble bas-relief. On the far left is the first group composed of four figures with, at the top, a warrior putting on a breastplate; on the far right is another, larger group, the top formed by the warrior with a shield, and the bottom by the nude hurriedly dressing. The dynamic composition of the painting becomes more evident at the centre where, in the foreground seeming almost to draw one towards the interior, there is an empty space boldly emphasized by the sudden twist of the nude body sitting on the ground, the legs lost in the melée. Above is the triangle formed by the two diverging nudes of warriors preparing for battle (one dressing, the other clutching a lance) who intersect and thus link the groups on either side.

Like Signorelli in Orvieto and Pollaiolo in his battles containing nude figures, Michelangelo has drawn an anthology of heroic nudes. Unlike his 15th-century predecessors, however, in Michelangelo's animated composition the anatomy of male bod-

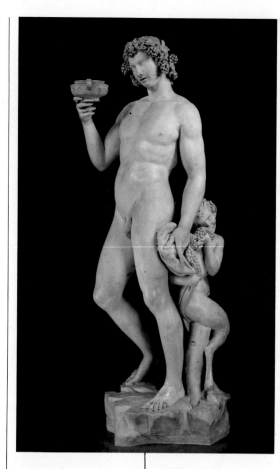

Bacchus
(1496-1497).
Florence,
Bargello Museum.

The statue was made in Rome for cardinal Raffaele Riario, cousin of the future pope Julius II. As with the small *Sleeping Cupid* (sold in Rome in 1496 as an antique) and the *Apollo Cupid* (both lost), Michelangelo created his own antique style, not strictly based on a specific model.

Right:
the *Doni Madonna*
(1506-1507),
detail after
restoration
(the complete work is
reproduced
on page 44).
Florence,
Galleria degli Uffizi.

Dying Slave
(1513).
Paris, Louvre.
**Also known
as the *Sleeping Slave*,
the figure was to have
been placed with
the *Rebellious Slave*
on the lower part
of Julius II's tomb.
Vasari interpreted
them historically
as representing the
provinces taken
by Julius II; Condivi
interpreted them
allegorically
as the liberal arts
lamenting the death
of the pope.
Within the funerary
monument the slaves
are clearly intended
to represent
a commemorative
element derived from
the classical
Triumphs.**

ies in movement, the taut muscles straining beneath the skin, is not merely superficial, but is produced by will, the effort of the spirit to transcend the body, to overcome the physical nature of the material with an entirely spiritual heroism.

Had it been completed, the fresco in Palazzo Vecchio, although entirely Florentine in character, would have been the immediate forerunner to the composition in the immense Sistine chapel. Michelangelo interrupted the work however, abandoning his beloved Florence for the Rome of Julius II. Demanding and authoritarian, the pope had summoned him to design the most ambitious project of the time – his own mausoleum which was to stand at the centre of Christianity's most important church, Saint Peter's.

Michelangelo devoted himself entirely to the new job: invited to Rome by the pope in March 1505 (probably on the advice of the Florentine, Giuliano da Sangallo), a contract was drawn up in the same month stipulating the enormous sum of 10,000 ducats and a period of five years in which to produce approximately forty statues, bas-reliefs in bronze and smaller figures. The following month the sculptor was already in Carrara to choose the most suitable marble and in January 1506 the blocks began to arrive in his workshop near Saint Peter's. For the tomb he not only abandoned the *Battle of Cascina*, but he also broke the contract for twelve statues of apostles for Santa Maria del Fiore. The monument for pope Julius was, he felt, the work in which he could best elaborate all the ideas, problems and forms teeming in his mind.

All we know of the original project is derived from descriptions provided by Vasari and Condivi, Michelangelo's earliest and most reliable biographers, though they are not always in agreement. Without doubt it was to have been a modulated, architectonic structure, free-standing rather than set against a wall like normal tombs, and placed centrally, probably in the chancel of the old Vatican church, over the tomb of Saint Peter. It was rectangular in form, eleven metres wide and seven deep, with three ascending orders each successively decreasing, almost like a pyramid. There was to be a small oval chamber inside, entered by one or perhaps two doors located in the centre of the longer side. On the lower order statues of Victory in two large flanking niches, and Prisoners or Slaves on square pilasters alluded to the virtues of the pope; in the middle order were statues of Moses, Saint Paul, the Active and the Contemplative Life; at the top, two allegorical figures (angels according to Condivi; heaven and earth for Vasari) support the coffin with a figure of Julius II.

It is more a grandiose Christian mausoleum than a tomb, rivalling the classical sepulchres of Roman emperors, or the mythical Mausoleum at Halicarnassus. The relationship between ancient and modern, between classical, heroic forms and Christian spirituality was inevitably seen very differently in the Roman than in the Florentine context.

In Rome, the classical, in all its lively ostentation, is a constantly vivid reality representing the historic foundation of the present, the supremacy of the Roman church over all others and the temporal power of the papacy which Julius forcefully imposed. It is useful to remember that Michelangelo was present when the statue of the *Laocoön* was rediscovered and that the Vatican church for which Michelangelo designed the tomb still consisted mainly of Constantine's imperial basilica.

The antique is history extracted from time, transcending it; according to Neoplatonism, Christian illumination reveals the most profound and intimate meaning of its pure form and discloses its intrinsic symbolism. The statues of Victory and the Slaves intended for the lower order of the tomb are antique forms

Above and below: Tolnay's reconstructions of the first (1505) and second (1513) designs for the Tomb of Julius II.

On the death of pope Julius II, Michelangelo abandoned the plan for a free-standing monument at the centre of the Vatican church, and decided to set the tomb against a wall, eliminating the internal space. The greater vertical emphasis is reinforced by the groups of statues at the corners and concludes in the figure of the Virgin and Child.

Above:
Tolnay's reconstruction of the third design (1516) for the Tomb of Julius II.
As in the contemporary designs for the façade of San Lorenzo, the formal problem is the relationship between architecture and sculpture.

Below: Tolnay's reconstruction of the fifth design (1532) for the Tomb of Julius II, designed for the church of San Pietro in Vincoli.
At this stage Michelangelo limits himself to making use of the statues already prepared.

Opposite page:
The Tomb of Julius II in the church of San Pietro in Vincoli.
The funerary monument to Julius II, as it was finally built, resulted from the contract of 1532. It was decided to place the structure in San Pietro in Vincoli using the sculptures already made _Moses_ (c. 1515) and various other architectural and decorative elements. The figures of _Rachel_ and _Leah_ were made in 1542 when the last contract was drawn up with the heirs of the former pope. Many collaborators worked on the final monument.

derived from the classical, imperial Triumphs and, at the same time, they symbolize the Resurrection, the Christian victory of the spirit over the physical, time and death. Although the little temple to Saint Peter at Montorio, a memorial on the place of martyrdom of the founder of the Roman church, was built during the same period, Bramante considers his monument as a 'genre', an obvious allegory of the historical rebirth of an antique style, recreated from the theory of Vitruvius' treatise and based on archeological evidence. Michelangelo, however, with his funerary structure to be built over the apostle's tomb, makes of his monument an ideal form which unites symbolically, and not allegorically, antiquity and christianity. The former is simply architecture, the latter the result of several techniques (architectural, sculptural and metal casting); for Michelangelo the monument, antique and modern at one and the same time, is a synthesis of the arts. He explains it thus: the form is not dictated by the material but is 'pre-existent' to it and is therefore unaffected by the technique used:

The best of artists hath no thought to show
Which the rough stone in its superfluous shell
Doth not include within its mass, and to this image arrives
Only the hand which is obedient to the mind.

Just as in sculpture the concept precedes the material and is brought into existence by removing the superfluous from the block of marble, in architecture the concept is realized by discarding the semantic code.

During this period Michelangelo, copying notebooks such as the _Corner Codex_, was studying the single classical architectural elements (capitals, bases, mouldings, pilaster strips), concentrating on their complex, and occasionally mysterious, morphology and ignoring the linguistic classifications which were considerable in the case of classicism. In the tomb therefore, the relationship between architecture and sculpture is not one of continuity or of technical contiguity, as it was later with Raphael, but of structural affinity combining to achieve a formal arrangement of several figures (human and architectural) within the space.

The project of 1505 was only the first chapter in what Michelangelo himself called the "tragedy of the tomb", a work which concerned him deeply, a catalyst of ideas later developed in other works, yet which proved impossible to complete. He blamed intrigue at the Roman court and the jealousy of the Urbino contingent, lead by Bramante and Raphael. The true reason was, in fact, an abrupt change in the plans of Julius II whose attention was seized by an even more ambitious project – the rebuilding of the Vatican church under the direction of Bramante. Michelangelo was incensed to see his plan set aside: in April, just before the foundation stone of the new Saint Peter's was to be laid, he left Rome and returned to Florence.

The reconciliation of these two strong personalities became an affair of state, requiring three papal briefs to the Florentine Signoria and the intervention of Soderini with the artist ("We don't want to go to war with the pope and put the whole of our State at risk for your sake") before Michelangelo could be convinced to meet Julius II, who was besieging Bologna, and ask to be forgiven. Most probably, rather than external pressure, he allowed himself to be persuaded by the assurance that the tomb was only temporarily delayed. The enormous bronze statue of Julius II placed on the façade of Bologna cathedral in February 1508 to celebrate the pope's victory over the rebellious city, and the result of a year's work, probably represents yet another experiment for the problematic tomb which continued to vex Michelangelo's thoughts.

The Sistine Chapel

Previous page:
lunette with
the inscription
«IACOB / IOSEPH»,
detail of a female
head (c. 1512).
Rome,
Sistine Chapel.

RELUCTANTLY, and still suspicious that his rivals were laying traps to diminish his reputation in the eyes of the pope, after completing the statue for Bologna (soon to be destroyed when the city again rebelled in 1511) he accepted the commission to fresco the ceiling of the Sistine chapel in the spring of 1508. He complained that he was not a painter and that the new work, of quite vast dimensions, would prevent him from completing pope Julius' tomb. Finally, in a note dated 10 May, he records that he has acquired an advance of 500 ducats for the job, "on which I will begin to work today".

The Great Chapel of the papal palace, first planned in the mid 15th century by Nicholas V as part of his vast programme of modernization of the Vatican, was built by Julius II's uncle, Sixtus IV, around 1475. Battisti proposed the suggestive theory that the proportions and architectural structure are based on those of Solomon's Temple. In his definitive analysis, Calvesi explained how the complex iconographic programme, probably suggested by the Franciscan pope himself, is based on the superiority of the Christian over the Jewish religion, of Christ over Moses, of the pope over Solomon, of the New Testament over the Old. Around the walls eight scenes from the life of Moses (on the left) corrispond to eight stories from the New Testament.

The conceptual density of the frescoes, painted between 1481 and 1482 by the most important artists active at the time in Umbria and Tuscany (not only Perugino, Pinturicchio and Signorelli, but also the Florentine Neoplatonist, Botticelli, one of Michelangelo's masters) deeply impressed the artist as well as Julius II who considered himself the perpetrator of his uncle's work. To replace the artificial starry sky painted by Pier Matteo d'Amelia, he at first thought of depicting twelve enormous figures of apostles on the corbels, and a simple architectural classical-style decoration in the central band of the vault (as can be seen in a drawing in the British museum and in another made only slightly later, now in Detroit). However, his plan soon became much more complex and cohesive probably, to provide a better relationship with the stories painted below. Instead of painted architecture, the large vault was divided into three vertical bands: in the highest band alternating large and small panels contain nine scenes from *Genesis*; to the sides of the smaller pan-

General view of the
vaulted ceiling
(1508-1512)
of the Sistine Chapel.

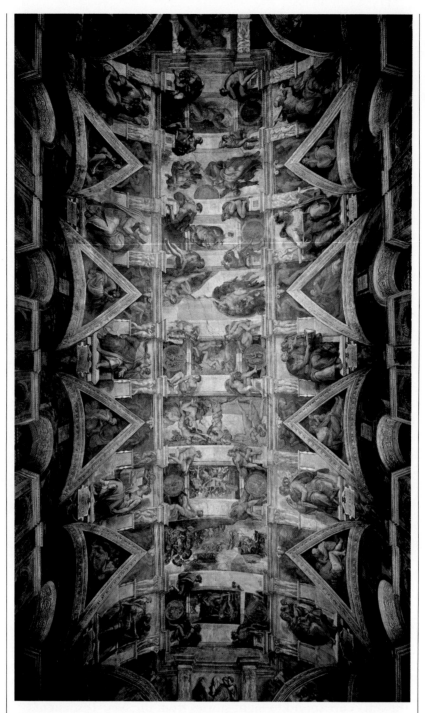

The structural
quality of the painted
architecture,
entirely lacking
any illusionistic
intention,
is quite evident.

els animated young male nudes hold fake bronze medallions
with further stories from the bible. Slightly lower, in the second
band, in the triangles which support the vault, Prophets and
Sibyls (the seers who have foretold the coming of the Lord) are
seated on thrones: in the lowest band, composed of triangles
and lunettes, are the forefathers of Christ and four heroes of
Israel who saved the Hebrew people, symbols of the promised
Messiah. While the relationship between these last two bands
and the scenes from the life of Moses and Christ is obvious, the
stories from *Genesis*, as Calvesi has pointed out, can also be seen
in terms of an 'introduction' to the 15th-century subjects below.
The vault conceived as an introduction, or preface, to the New
Testament scenes also explains its general character: what did
Michelangelo really want to paint? What precisely does the vault
represent, not in its single, descriptive scenes, but in its overall
significance?
      Re-examining the work after the recent restoration, the

structural role of the architecture clearly emerges; with the heavy layer of dirt and grease now removed, the close, fundamental, relationship with the human figures is quite evident, as indeed it was also intended to be in Pope Julius' tomb. Firstly it was not 'real' architecture, a design to be seen from below, as were the ceilings painted in Rome by Mantegna (later unfortunately destroyed, though in the early 16th century they certainly provided models). The corbels on which the nudes rest diverge, and do not refer to the some vanishing point; even in the thrones of the Seers the varying depths are contradictory. Lying beyond the architecture, at the two far ends, is a blue sky matching that in the stories of *Genesis* which consequently do not have the appearance of framed pictures, although the minor stories are surrounded by architectural mouldings. Even in the biblical scenes there are no relationships of a proportional-perspective nature; there are neither structures nor objects to give depth and provide a rational sense of space as there were in the 15th century paintings below, especially in the scenes where Christ is represented. Everything in the ceiling seems to reject not only spatial limits but also the normal, exact rules of light. The shadows, as the restoration has clearly revealed, seem to be attributes of the individual figure, and thus quite independent of any environmental factors.

Yet how can we describe an image which so blatantly, almost programmatically, ignores the laws of light and space? It is a 'vision', as is the *Pietà* in the Vatican, which is not conditioned by the emotions, but is stimulated by the less deceptive and more reliable eye of the intellect. As a Neoplatonic 'visio intellectualis', no longer a 're-presentation', but a 'presentiment', the ceiling of the Sistine is precisely the opposite of the visions portrayed only a few years later by Correggio, traditionally considered to be the intermediary between Leonardo and Baroque illusionism, in which the extraterrestrial materializes in a natural form in the present, to the increasing horror of the observer. In Michelangelo things do not proceed according to nature, but according to the law of internal contradiction, the matching of opposites. The mind associates facts distant in time, but connected by a philosophical-rational order: the Seers foresee and are therefore contemporary to the event they predict; the Flood and the drunkeness of Noah are preludes to the coming of Christ and therefore are part of it; the nudes are classic in form because they relate to the events in the ceiling. Associating the two events annuls the time which has passed between them, just as foreshortening annuls the space between two separate and distant points, relating the closest to the furthest distance.

In the same way that foreshortening is the removal of the rules governing perspective in order to provide a clearer image, so the extraordinary brilliance revealed with the cleaning of the lunettes is, quite simply, the removal of the rules governing natural lighting. Strident pairs of opposing yet complementary colours which cannot intermingle, such as yellow and blue, red, purple and green, stand out in the full purity of their colour tone without any gradually shaded transition. It is a concept which can only be considered polemical when compared to Leonardo's shades and nuances which mingle and combine only "friend" colours as propounded by Alberti. Recent restoration of the *Doni Madonna*, painted in Florence around 1507, has removed the thick yellow varnish and has revealed the same technique, the same splendid crystal-clear colours of the Sistine chapel, the same underlying theory of contrast, later a model for Rosso Fiorentino and Pontormo, the same heroic classicism in the male nudes.

Ruth and Obed, lunette between the *Persian Sibyl* and the *Prophet Jeremiah* (c. 1512). Rome, Sistine Chapel.

Restoration revealed the clarity of the original colours.

The return to Florence

Opposite page:
Tomb of Lorenzo
de' Medici.
Florence,
San Lorenzo,
New Sacristy.

WHILE THE CEILING OF the Sistine chapel is clearly the greatest achievement of Michelangelo's youthful works, the *Last Judgement* painted on the far wall of the same chapel is the fundamental embodiment of his mature works. Between the two, however, he spent a lengthy period in Florence, still working on plans for the tomb of Julius II, the façade and New Sacristy of San Lorenzo, the Biblioteca Laurenziana and lastly plans for the city's fortifications. None of the later plans for the tomb of Julius (the second was made in 1513, the third in 1516, the fourth in 1526, the fifth in 1532 and the last was actually constructed in 1545) consisted of a free-standing entity, nor had an internal chamber: the model was no longer the classical mausoleum, but a Christian sepulchre as conceived in the Middle Ages. The experience of the Sistine chapel and the failure of the first project seem to have erased any enthusiasm for the antique, the problem of history and the synthesis of the arts. The *Slaves* in the Louvre, begun in Rome in 1513 for the second project of the tomb, are evidence of the transition: they are still based on antique models, but the heroic ideal is no longer the classical nude but rather Saint Sebastian, the Christian warrior. Lightly sculpted with colour and light, the forms emerge painfully from the stone which takes on a metaphysical quality. The *Christ* of the Minerva is an Apollo expressive of contrasting classicism: the cross and instruments of the Passion are shown not as attributes of Triumph, but in the awareness that martyrdom is suffered at the hands of men. During the same period Sebastiano del Piombo portrayed a similar style of sacred image in some of his paintings such as the *Pietà* and the *Flagellation*, probably based on drawings and with the advice of Michelangelo himself.

He no longer relates to the elderly Leonardo, but rather the younger Raphael and his thriving school. Quite distant, despite being in the same palace, the ceiling in the Sistine chapel and the rooms decorated contemporarily for Julius II, reveal differences that are more evident in the two competing projects for the façade of San Lorenzo. Comparison of the two designs (Michelangelo's long recognized, Raphael's recently discovered by Tafuri) shows that the debate between the two artists concerned the interaction of the various arts and the nature of language. According to Raphael's thesis the institution of language

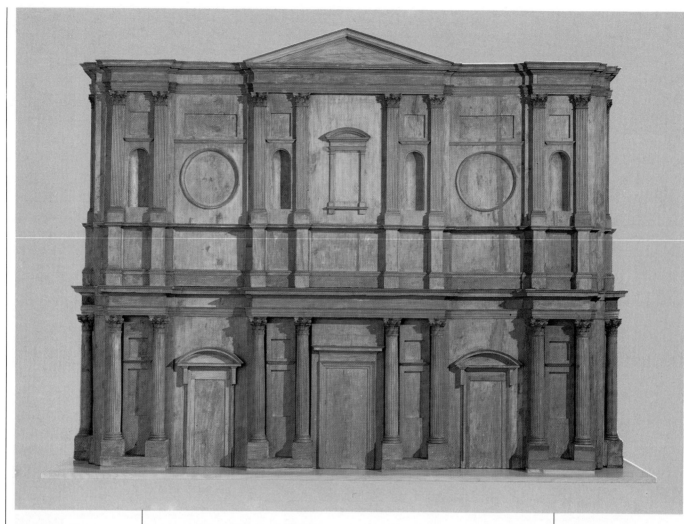

Wooden model
for the façade
of San Lorenzo
(c. 1519).
Florence,
Casa Buonarroti.

was based on conventions, as in Aristotle, while, according to
Michelangelo, it developed directly out of nature, as in Plato. In
prose terms the former corresponds to an artificially constructed
Italian selected from the various dialects of the peninsula; the latter prefers the superiority of Tuscany's Dante, Petrarch and
Boccaccio. Identified in a copy made by Aristotle da Sangallo,
Raphael's project is an elegant exercise based on the sophistica-
tions of architectural vocabulary: the past is represented by the
authority of Vitruvius and is confirmed by the study of Roman
ruins, thus justifying neologisms and licences; sculpture and
architecture are two arts with their own autonomous conventions. The façade designed by Michelangelo, who sees it as "architecture and sculpture to mirror all of Italy", is quite independent
of Brunelleschi's interior; it is a pliant structure not dependent
on, but in complete harmony with the sculpture, sharing its
intrinsic essence as an existential expression.

In the New Sacristy of San Lorenzo architecture and sculpture are equal protagonists. Michelangelo evokes the old sacristy
designed by Brunelleschi almost a century earlier, but while in
the 15th-century version the walls were simply open surfaces, geometric sections of a general perspective, here they become limit-
ing factors, inhibited by the emphatic framework of the arches
and pilaster strips (and the unusual jambs against which these are
set). Forced out of these enclosed spaces, as if by compression,
are the tombs and architectural elements, the highly modulated
aediculas, the windows of the attic (a complete innovation with
respect to Brunelleschi) tapering sharply upwards, the string-
courses projecting outwards like bolsters.

In such an 'unnatural' setting, illuminated by light entering

**Despite several
differences
to the contract
of 1518,
the model,
as James Ackerman
has shown,
is very similar
to Michelangelo's
design.**

diagonally from the windows (higher on the outside than on the inside) and reflecting on the marble of the walls, it is not surprising that the majestic decoration should be so imposing, not only the architectural features but also the stucco work and frescoes by Giovanni da Udine, destroyed in the 16th century.

The revolutionary novelty of the decoration, indicative of the profound 'anti-naturalism' of Michelangelo's design, was noted by Vasari who wrote, "he did the ornamentation in a composite order, in a style more varied and more original than any other master, ancient or modern, has ever been able to achieve. For the beautiful cornices, capitals, bases, doors, tabernacles and tombs were extremely novel, and in them he departed a great deal from the kind of architecture regulated by proportion, order, and rule which other artists did according to common usage and following Vitruvius and the works of antiquity but from which Michelangelo wanted to break away".

That this was not mere licence is shown by the Biblioteca Laurenziana, the exception which serves to prove the rule. Here too Michelangelo applies his equation 'architecture equals energy' which is repressed in the reading room but bursts out into the vestibule from where the staircase seems to explode from above, expanding forcibly into the small space which contains the eruption. The columns are pressed violently into the walls, pushing them back and giving them form, the mouldings jut out arrogantly beneath the weight of the stairway, the steps of which curve emphasizing further the notion of expansion; the disproportionate height of the vestibule is violently contracted. The rare books room, a tranquil place for study and reflection intended to be situated beyond the reading room, was to be a triangular space with highly defined walls, checking and counterbalancing the impetuosity of the landing, mediating between the verticality of the vestibule and the horizontality of the reading room, demonstrating that a single space can be defined by many different forms.

The project for the fortifications of Florence was the last commission Michelangelo undertook for his city. The Medici were expelled in 1527 and the republican government assigned him the task of improving the city's defence in anticipation of the inevitable retaliation. Reflecting on the noble qualities of a people at war in defence of their liberty, he designed gates and ramparts concentrating on the aggressive action of the artillery, rather than on the static concept of protecting the defenders. The resulting structures, built to facilitate the differing trajectories of fire and conceived as sources emitting energy, consequently had an internal dynamism and almost anthropomorphic forms: rising, claw-like curves ready to trap and devour the enemy, crab-like ramparts positioned on the hillsides to obstruct the attackers, pulsating star-shaped buildings shooting geometric fire.

The quarrels, the continual suspicion of betrayal which circulated amongst the city's defenders, the lengthy seige (from October 1529 to the following August), fear of the Medici reprisal, all deeply affected Michelangelo. After fleeing to Venice he returned to Florence to take part in the final effort of resistance. With the city now invaded by imperial troops he was hunted by assassins and forced to go into hiding while his republican friends were hanged or imprisoned until, in exchange for completing the work on San Lorenzo, he was pardoned by Clement VII in November.

It was, however, the end of an epoch as well as of a profound experience. A few years later, after the death of the Medici pope, Michelangelo left Florence once more, returning, this time permanently, to Rome still recovering from the sack of 1527. In the meantime Paul III had been elected pope.

Top:
Day (1526-1531),
detail of the tomb
of Giuliano
de' Medici.
Florence,
San Lorenzo,
New Sacristy.

Above:
Dawn (1524-1527),
detail of the tomb
of Lorenzo
de' Medici.
Florence,
San Lorenzo,
New Sacristy.

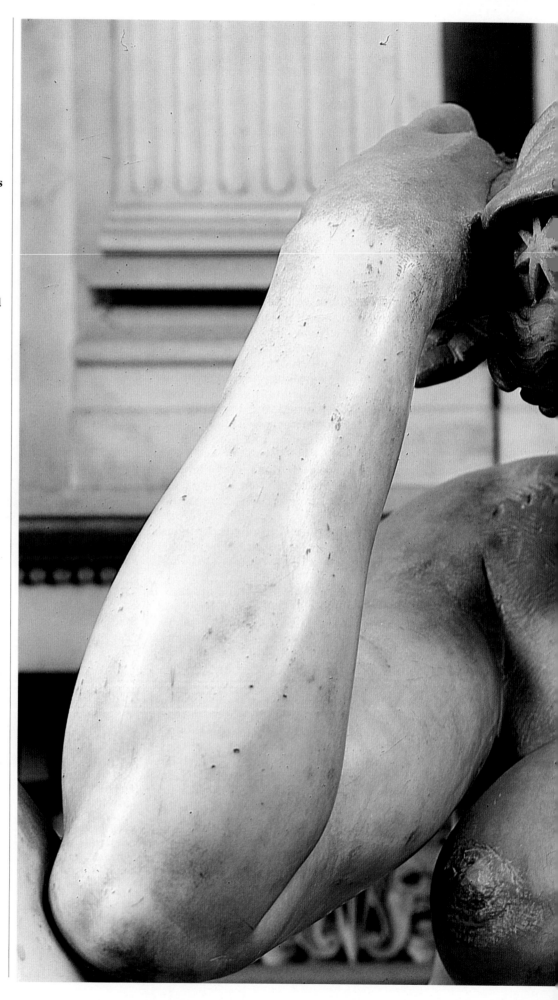

Night
(1526-1531),
detail,
Florence,
San Lorenzo,
New Sacristy.
**The statue
is on the left side
of the tomb
of Giuliano
de' Medici
and was one
of the first sculptures
made for the Medici
tombs.
The pose,
with the head resting
on the hand,
was used
by Michelangelo
in other works,
such as the destroyed
Leda, and probably
alludes
to melancholy.**

The papacy of Paul III

THE TASK OF DECORATING the far wall of the Sistine chapel was probably assigned to Michelangelo in 1533, but he only began work three years later, on being released by a papal motu proprio from his obligations to the heirs of Julius II for the time required to complete the new work. Unlike the vault, a painted architecture was not used here to harmonize the physical space with the frescoed scene. On the contrary the lunettes painted in 1512 were eliminated, together with Perugino's *Assumption* beneath, to avoid constricting the images within an architectural framework, giving it the appearance of a framed picture. Thus the wall suggested a huge empty page, like the inner façades of Medieval churches.

There is no more a synthesis of the arts and of the ancient and modern: human history is brought to an end with an imperious gesture of Christ the Judge, the definitive arbiter of good and evil, of salvation and eternal forgiveness. These are the themes that produced the Christian ecumenical schism which, at the time, could no longer be considered as simply an argument between an ingenuous German Augstinian monk and learned papal theologians. The sack of Rome in 1527 had shown how strong Lutheran teaching had become and the widespread hatred of Rome and of the papacy had succeeded in violating the Eternal City, its monuments, until now studied and admired, and its relics, once venerated and respected.

In painting a theme of such theological importance and content, Michelangelo had no help nor advisors, he did not illustrate religious tracts, and used no other sources than the Bible and his "most familiar" Dante. He was, however, in contact with Vittoria Colonna and supporters of catholic reform who emphasized the importance of faith in the process of salvation. He did not even consider using the accepted iconographic tradition which portrayed Christ enthroned on high, surrounded by his court of saints and angels, with the chosen lower on the right and the condemned on the left.

On first sight the *Last Judgement* seems not to have any structure, as if it were the shapeless product of an explosion: groups of figures eddy and whirl around Christ the Judge, surrounded and isolated by a luminous aura amidst wide spaces of blue sky. Only gradually do we realise that the seething groups have a circular direction, beginning on the left, from where the chosen rise slowly,

Marcello Venusti,
Last Judgement.
Naples,
Museo
di Capodimonte.
Copy
of Michelangelo's
fresco before
Daniele da Volterra's
alterations (1564).

Last Judgement (1537-1541). Rome, Sistine Chapel.

Comparison with Venusti's work reveals the alterations made after the Council of Trent (January 1564) as well as the darkening of the original colours.

*Conversion
of Saint Paul*
(1542-1545).
Rome,
Vatican Palace,
Pauline Chapel.

drawn upwards by Christ's gesture, while His left arm is sending the damned to the depths. Thus everything revolves around the figure of God in judgement, Nomos, Law, just as the faces of the saints, the Virgin's timid gesture of intercession and the weighty instruments of the Passion clutched threateningly by the angels, all converge on Him. As in a sacred oration, the entire piece can only succeed if founded on a powerful rhythm: there is no perspective nor tonal harmony, the clusters of nudes meet and separate, they clash and rebound subjected to the twin poles of attraction, high-low, heaven-earth, Christ-hell, they are arranged on spatial axes diverging from the large central space, yet co-ordinated by the figure of Christ-Apollo.

The same concept can be seen in the contemporary re-organization of the Campidoglio: co-ordination between the diverging axes of the two palaces was obtained with the pattern of interwoven elipses in the pavement and the monumental stairway which extended into the piazza to provide a rapport with Palazzo Senatorio, while the empty depth of the portico was connected to the jutting cornice above by the order of colossal pilasters.

Not only are the nudes of the *Judgement* painted without per-

*Crucifixion
of Saint Peter*
(1545-1560).
Rome,
Vatican Palace,
Pauline Chapel.

Below:
Stairway
of Palazzo Senatorio
(c. 1540).
Rome,
Campidoglio.
**The stairway
is one of the few
elements for which
Michelangelo
was without doubt
entirely responsible.
Palazzo
dei Conservatori
was in fact made
by Giacomo
della Porta
to a design
by Michelangelo,
while
Palazzo Nuovo
was built
the following century.**

spective or chromatic harmony, but the figures now also lack both the classical dignity of those in the ceiling and the elegant, elongated proportions of the Florentine period (such as in the *Victory* in Palazzo Vecchio). They are now directly expressive of the situation or the existential condition of the person: the bodies of the damned are earthy, heavy, plastered with mud, the expressions of the demons are vulgar and grotesque, the chosen are more lithe and slender, the saints heroic but not proud, appalled by the horror of the event. If the *Judgement* of the Sistine chapel, official centre of Christendom, representative of papal authority, is a religious public oration, the two frescoes painted for the private chapel of Paul III are pure, sacred lyricism. Terror for the relentlessness of the Law and the awareness of authority and justice are succeeded by examples of conversion and martyrdom, two fundamental elements of Christian experience. They could well have been portrayed as two historic events, but history is bound to the living world and in the place where the pope meditated and communed with God, the worldly had no right to enter. The conversion of Paul and the martyrdom of Peter are not here edifying examples nor admonishments to lead a life of religion, but are rather reminders of the heavy responsibilities of the representative who, on election to the throne of Peter, has chosen the name of Paul. In Saul's conversion the centre (unfilled space in the *Judgement*) is an eddying void, almost as in the *Battle of Cascina*. The horse is fleeing towards the distance and foreshortening brings the sky and distant hills immediately into the foreground. Everything is brought forward, almost spilling over the edge of the painted surface where Saul's heavy body is seen supported with difficulty by two figures. From on high, also audaciously foreshortened, Christ descends in a blaze of light which does not impart natural illumination to the scene, but only emphasizes the vertical break in the composition. On both sides, in heaven and in earth, the angels and onlookers move aside, straining outwards, leaving space for the meeting between

God and Paul. Everything in the *Conversion* expresses the fearful, overwhelming presence of God; the *Crucifixion of Saint Peter* shows the desolation of His absence. The horizon is high and distant, the action takes place on the ground, there is barely room for the sky. Unlike the martyrs of the counter-reform and the Baroque period (filled with floating angels holding palms, with God on high welcoming those who merit forgiveness amongst the blessed), here Peter is alone, there is no certainty at the time of his death of another life, his agony is a tragic and solitary spiritual experience, the ultimate trial of the Christian soul. The air seems almost breathless; the silent throng of onlookers does not form a theatrical scene, but actually emphasizes Peter's solitude. The fulcrum of the scene is the splendid figure of the man digging – recalling the continual reference to Masaccio – crouching on the ground making the hole where the cross will be placed. Opposing and balancing the curve of the body, Peter turns on the cross and his movement towards the left and the right is extended and continued by his torturers forming a wide crescent, counterbalanced by the sharp foreshortening of the cross, slanting diagonally across the entire painting and linking heaven and earth. As far as one can judge after much earlier restoration, the colours are sharp, strident, acrid, clashing; the hue of the paint no longer emanates from the body, nor is it a means for the surface to react to light, but is a spiritual essence, a tint which could even suggest its opposite, complete elimination, a total absence of colour, the final evidence, almost like a larva, of the body abandoned. The chapel of Paul III thus represents the final and definitive statement of Michelangelo's refusal to consider art as Aristotelian mimesis, merely a representative imitation of reality.

The later years

Opposite page:
plan for the church
of San Giovanni
dei Fiorentini
in Rome (1559).
Florence,
Casa Buonarroti.
**In Michelangelo's
later architectural
designs a dynamic
composition based
on the diagonal
placing of the axes
is evident.**

Vault of the Sforza
Chapel (1559).
Rome, Santa Maria
Maggiore.

THE PAINTINGS IN
Pope Paul's chapel were the last; Michelangelo stopped painting,
as he announced in a letter to Vasari, affirming that it was an activity unsuitable for old men. Aged seventy-five when he finished the
Crucifixion, he was indeed elderly. More than anything however,
after the Pauline chapel only the sublime could follow. Moreover,
after the disappointment of Julius II's tomb, constructed in San
Pietro in Vincoli in 1545, and the *Brutus,* now in the Bargello,
which displays all the moral force of the figures in the *Last
Judgement,* sculpture too became an entirely private activity, an intimate reflection on his own death as in the last, harrowing *Pietà.*
Architecture, which has no need of the unreliable and treacherous
figurative, is the sublime art; consequently he completed the plans
for San Giovanni dei Fiorentini, the Sforza chapel in Santa Maria
Maggiore, Porta Pia, Santa Maria degli Angeli and Saint Peter's.

The first two are variations on the Renaissance tradition of
the central plan to which Michelangelo gives a dynamic force with
crossed axes, rather than basing it on the harmony of regular, geo-

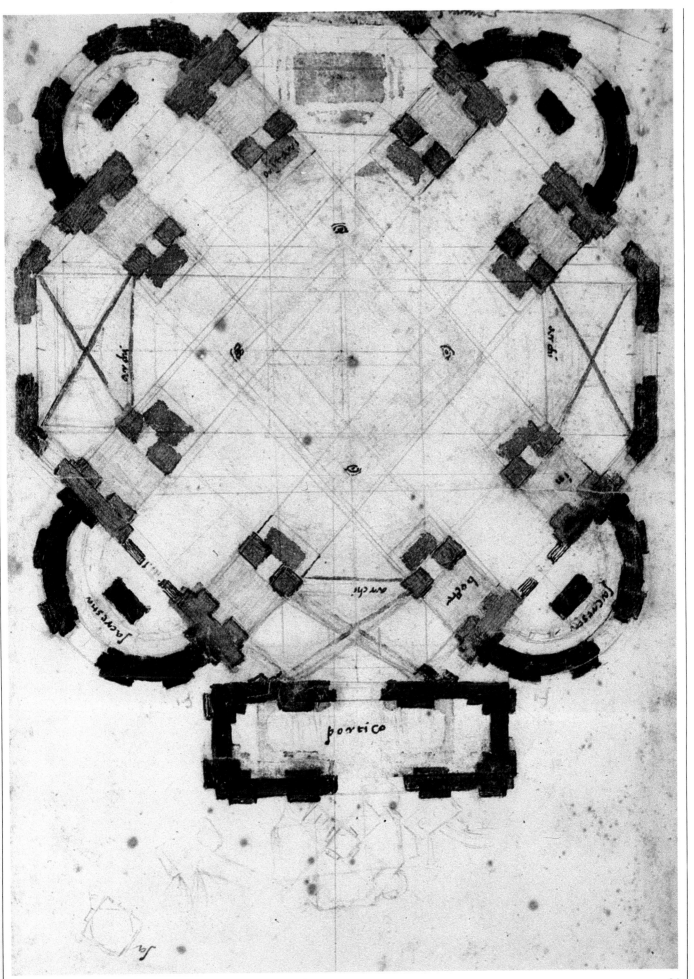

porti co

Left:
The Basilica
of Saint Peter's,
view of the dome.
**Only the drum
was made during
Michelangelo's life.
The problem
of the dome,
in particular
the profile
of the curve,
greatly perplexed
him during the
last years of his life.
The vault
and the lantern were
made by Giacomo
della Porta.**

Above:
Porta Pia
(1561) in Rome.

metric forms. His many studies for San Giovanni dei Fiorentini suggest the expansion of the central area into the perimetrical spaces of the chapels and entrance, which thus formed and modelled the surfaces of the walls. In the Sforza chapel the diagonal cross of two axes brings the columns forward dramatically into the central space so that it is clutched in an iron grip. In Porta Pia only the doorway and the blind windows were of interest to him (other details were simply added by inexpert followers) the neutral surface of the façade being seen as nothing more than a stone screen continuing the pre-existing walls. It is an outright denunciation of the absurdity of architectural language: how might the improbable order of the doorway be classified? Moreover, the substitution of freestanding columns with grooved pilaster strips is the ultimate rejection of any similarity between architecture and sculpture. Seen from a distance, as though it were a stage set or backdrop, the doorway appears flattened, becoming two-dimensional, the light modulates its shape.

The last works undertaken by the elderly Michelangelo - the cupola of Saint Peter's and Santa Maria degli Angeli - are the most awe-inspiring. The tectonics of the former contrast with the 'anti-architecture' of the latter, the 'great disgrace and sin' of leaving the one incomplete contrasts with the almost symbolic contribution to the other, modifying the appearance and arrangement with only minimal alterations to the walls and the lighting. The wave of Lutheranism had, in fact, derived from the scandal concerning the selling of indulgences, proceeds from which were intended to finance the building of the new basilica. Later, Antonio da Sangallo the younger had managed to make a sinecure for himself, as well as an income for his entire entourage, with the building of Saint Peter's. In 1546, reluctantly accepting the appointment as chief architect, Michelangelo imposed the condition that he would work without pay. With the simplest of alterations he transformed the existing building, restoring unity to the fragmentary elements of Sangallo's work. He returned to Bramante's central plan only modifying the design to accentuate the form of the masses. The dome was the ultimate reference to Florence and the humanist tradition; from the beginning Santa Maria del Fiore represented the model and Michelangelo even requested the exact dimensions of the dome. While Brunelleschi had raised his 'high over the heavens', with a form representative of the universe, Michelangelo conceived his dome above Saint Peter's as symbolizing the tension between man and God. It begins at the cross of the central plan, is carried upwards by the convergence of the lateral arms, taut and tense as springs. It finally rises from a drum which gains rotational force from the pairs of columns giving rise to sixteen ribs, double the number on Brunelleschi's dome in order to reduce the inert surface of each segment and emphasize the counter-thrust effect of the raised ribs. The problem of the curvature plagued Michelangelo and he developed several solutions though he left his final decision until the last possible moment. The problem lay not so much in the curvature as in the relationship between dome and lantern, which has to contain, control and balance the thrust without, however, reducing it. This is the final act in the drama of Julius II's tomb, which should have stood in the basilica beneath. To have left it unfinished would have meant humiliation, conclusive defeat in a life entirely identified with art, and for an art entirely identified with the flow of existence.

Worried by his advancing age, anxious to define and conclude the project for the tomb and aware that it was impossible to express a highly sculptural concept in sketches or plans, he made a model in clay, followed by a larger one in wood. He finished the work in November 1561 and, less than three years later, he died.

Michelangelo artist and poet

Giulio Carlo Argan

Copy
of the *Tribute Money*
by Masaccio in the
Brancacci chapel,
Santa Maria
del Carmine
in Florence
(1488-1495).
Munich,
Kupferstich Kabinett.

Following page:
*The Abduction
of Ganymede,*
(c. 1530).
Cambridge,
(Massachussets),
Fogg Art Museum.

ichelangelo was, without doubt, one of the most important founders of Mannerism, yet he was even more explicitly a Mannerist in his poetry than in his painting or sculpture where the impact of originality and an amazing bravura of technique eclipse the scrupulous accuracy of the written word. Michelangelo was first recognized as one of the greatest poets of the 16th century by Walter Binni who saw that the deeply intense existential experience and the genuine and incessantly turbulent conflict between ardent eroticism and a desperate religious fervour are evident with even greater clarity in the finely cut facets of verse. Binni, moreover, analysed the relationship between the poems and the letters, obviously written without any attempt at elegance of style, thus revealing 'Michelangelo the writer' – a poet though not a man of letters. The artist himself frequently asserted that he was no man of letters, and with none of the false modesty with which he claimed not to be an architect or even a painter. He did have a literary education: his earliest poems show the direct influence of Poliziano, Lorenzo de' Medici's popular poems, as well as a certain religious element, derived from Savonarola and Benivieni. He read and re-read the great 14th-century authors, Dante and Petrarch, and was able to compare and occasionally skilfully combine, the two styles. Throughout his lengthy artistic production as sculptor, painter and architect he never ceased to write poetry. The first known compositions date from 1502, the last just before 1560. Depending on the work on hand, he wrote more in some periods, less in others and the fact that many of the poems are written on pages alongside drawings and sketches would seem to suggest a close link between the figurative and the poetic work. The relationship is clearly casual and may also be infrequent, yet it reveals, in visual form, a certain parallelism, or at least similarity, in attempting to clarify and define what he referred to as a 'concept'. It is quite logical that, no less than sculptural and pictorial representation, poetry could demonstrate the artist's own awareness of the contradictions which constitute the dynamism of his philosophy – respect for authority yet the need to question it, censure and transgression, equally intense mysticism and eroticism, pride and self mortification. It is quite clear that the relationship is not that of 'ut pictura poësis' as suggested by Clements. Michelangelo does not say the same things using different forms; what he expresses in words cannot be expressed in

Filippo Brunelleschi, dome of Santa Maria del Fiore, Florence.

the same way with visual images and, as he believes thought to be a total unity, poetry represents the value of the word, of names and terms, within the unity of his conceptual system. Deciding whether the role of the word had greater or lesser value is irrelevant; what matters is to understand that it is intrinsic, that in fact his sculpture and his painting would have been different if the physical sculptural or pictorial image were not somehow affected by the precision of the word or name and that the word must somehow have been influenced by the visual image.

The problem may therefore be seen in its historic context.

During the 15th and early 16th century, the debate concerning language was one of the principle concerns of Humanist culture. At a most fundamental level, the choice between Latin and the Italian language represents the basic problem of defining the means of expression and communication of a society which, considering itself modern, desired renewal. Its modernity was quite different to the emphatically modern, technical and international style which had come into being in the 14th century with the development and spread of the Gothic. On the contrary it did not reject its relationship with the past, except as an almost hereditary perpetrator of an ancient culture whose authority was recognized, at least formally, a priori.

Humanistic culture was that of a bourgeoisie which aspired to

The dome of Florence cathedral completed the plan by Arnolfo di Cambio who first began the building of the church. Brunelleschi's design transformed the Gothic building into a highly modulated form which entirely dominates the surrounding space.

External view of the apse of the Baptistery of San Giovanni in Florence.

political power and cultural control and thus rejected tradition which implied an absolute recognition of the principle of authority: it sought instead an intentional and voluntary rediscovery of the antique – a return to the source. True modernity did not consist simply of current progress and development, the refining and perfecting of a tradition; rather, it was based on direct and genuine knowledge of, and comparison with, the antique. When Brunelleschi built the dome of Santa Maria del Fiore, inventing a technique not identical but comparable to that used in classical times, it was not progress but a veritable revolution compared to the highly advanced building technique which had developed with international Gothic. It was logical that in rejecting the modernism of international Gothic (French and German therefore) one should return to the Latinate source. The form was no longer universal, however, but assumed a local identity, not even derived from Rome, now in an irrevocable state of decay and neglect, but from Florence: for Brunelleschi the form closest to antique architecture was Florentine Romanesque.

Clearly, from the beginning the problem of language as verbal communication was considered as equal to that of art as visual communication. Leon Battista Alberti formulated, or at least theorized the new concept of art as knowledge; he was, moreover an important defender of the dignity of literature and of the poetic

The geometric arrangement of the structure, characteristic of Florentine Romanesque, is similar to the architectural style of the later classical period.

Left:
Madonna of the Steps
(1490-1492).
Florence,
Casa Buonarroti.
**The reference
to Donatello
is clear in the use
of very low relief;
a technique whose
dramatic,
expressive possibili-
ties Michelangelo
exploited
to the full.
The figure
of the Virgin
in the foreground
shows a greater
familiarity
with classical
sculpture.**

possibilities of Italian language. His treatise on painting is dated 1436 and the first competition for vernacular poetry, the *Certame Coronario* was held in 1441. It should also be remembered that Alberti was probably the greatest influence on Michelangelo's artistic education in particular.

During the first half of the 16th century the debate over language involved almost all Italian men of letters: it was a crucial problem not only of the culture but of the society of the day and it could certainly not be seen merely in terms of a choice, by now superfluous, between the pedantic defenders of Latin and the more enlightened supporters of the vernacular. Even earlier than Bembo, an authoritative mediator between the two currents, Erasmus had realized that the complexity of Christian ethics, philosophy, and modern scientific research could no longer be fully and effectively expressed in the language of a great, but extinct, civilization. It is true that it had been resuscitated, but the resurrection of Lazzarus demonstrates the divine power of Christ, not the immortality of Lazzarus. It was logical that Latin should remain the language of the Church, possibly of all institutions worth preserving – it was the language of authority. Italian was the language of freedom and action, but where did its historic roots and linguistic structure lie? – In the persuasive rhetoric of Cicero's discourses, the conceptual density of Dante, the narrative vivacity of Boccaccio, the phonetic harmony of Petrarch or even in the written transcription of the spoken language as in Aretino's *Ragionamenti?*

Michelangelo did not himself participate in the debate on language, but he was clearly aware of it. In any case the debate soon spread from the field of literature to that of the figurative arts. Humanist art naturally admired and identified with ancient Roman art – it was to art as Latin was to language. What was the relationship of the ancient with the modern? For architecture the problem was even more complex: its entire vocabulary derived from the antique. Could a new architecture develop from ancient terms? And if antique forms developed into new architecture using a new syntax, what changes would it make to the forms derived from the antique? Was this not also a problem of language?

The problem of language, especially in the light of the extreme dignity which Dante and Petrarch had given to the Italian tongue, was inevitably linked to the hotly disputed question of Florentine vernacular's identification with literary Italian language. Political interests, rather than linguistic or literary, had provoked Machiavelli to write his *Dialogo intorno alla nostra lingua.* The tense, yet inevitable, relationship between classicism and Florence had

Donatello,
*Saint George
and the Dragon*
(c. 1420),
on the base made
for the statue
of *Saint George.*
Florence, Bargello
Museum
(originally
in Orsanmichele).

Leonardo frequently portrayed the theme of the Virgin and Child, Saint Ann and Saint John the Baptist. In the cartoon in the National Gallery he recreates the classic image of beauty not only in the faces of the two women, whom Berenson defined as "Praxitelean", but also in the perfect balance of the composition. Delicate shading harmoniously relates the figures within the physical setting.

been the constant theme of Donatello's sculpture from the early decades of the 15th century. Michelangelo, a direct descendant via Bertoldo, never ceased to admire this aspect and demonstrated his perfect appreciation of it in the *Madonna of the Steps*, an early bas-relief in which he unites the grandeur of the classical with the powerful and entirely Florentine terseness of Donatello's extremely low relief. Not only the affection for his father and brothers and the pride in his aristocratic, though impoverished, family, but indeed his entire artistic output, including and perhaps especially his Roman works, demonstrate his clear, and even

Leonardo da Vinci,
*Virgin and Child,
Saint Ann and Saint
John the Baptist*
(c. 1499).
London ,
National Gallery.

The example
of Leonardo
influenced an entire
generation
of Florentine painters
from Fra Bartolomeo
to Andrea del Sarto.
It also affected
the work of both
Michelangelo
and Raphael.
Various of
Michelangelo's
compositions
are concerned with
the representation
of a group of figures
within a space such
as the *Pitti Madonna*
and the *Taddei
Madonna* as well
as the painting
of the *Doni Madonna*.
In the frequently
repeated theme
of the Madonna and
Child and the Holy
Family, Raphael,
who came to
Florence in 1504,
sought a synthesis
of Micheangelo
and Leonardo's
divergent ideas.

*Virgin and Child,
Saint Ann and Saint
John the Baptist*
(1501).
Oxford,
Ashmolean Museum.
**Michelangelo's
drawing reproduces
Leonardo's style.**

defiant, desire to be and to remain, Florentine.

This is just as evident in his poetic works, where the rather frequent and certainly intentional vernacular expressions and the sharp syntactic contractions are most blatantly Florentine. It was not in his nature to use them purely for colourful effect.

Why then did he write poetry, denying at the same time that he was a man of letters? At the beginning at least the reason may have been entirely casual. Michelangelo was always observant of his contemporaries and, although he was not fond of him, especially of Leonardo whom he recognized to be as capable as himself. One

Last Judgement
(1537-1541),
detail showing
the Resurrection
of the flesh.
Rome,
Sistine Chapel.

reason for the tension between the two was Leonardo's 'betrayal' of Florence for Milan in 1481; on a deeper level, however, lay the close relationship Leonardo saw between art and scientific research, his use of drawing as experiment and study instead of a definitive formal outline, his belief that nature was an indeterminate reality, a problem to study rather than a difficulty to overcome. Leonardo's forms certainly had no verbal equivalent; they lacked precisely that which Michelangelo strove to attain – the condition of absolute unity of spirit whereby the visual image contained both the concept and the act, and where the concept and the act were immediately and entirely evident in the visual image. Certainly, for Michelangelo painting was not silent poetry; painting and poetry were two different forms of eloquence and perhaps he wrote poetry precisely to emphasize the difference.

Later on it was Raphael who provided the terms of comparison. Although he accepted the need for a relationship between visual and verbal expression he was more interested in the demonstrative articulation of speech than in the distilled conceptuality of the word. In fact, while Raphael's model was Cicero's rhetoric, Michelangelo's was Dante's 'vulgaris eloquentia'. The difference is even more pronounced considering that Michelangelo and

The concept of space
in Raphael
is the epitome of the
study of harmony
and the triumphant
rediscovery
of the classical world.
In the *Universal
Judgement*, almost thirty years later than the
Stanze, space has
been
transformed into
a spiralling dynamism
within which
the terrifying
figure of Christ
in Judgement arises.
The theme
is traditionally Tuscan
(Signorelli)
and the ferocious
images are derived
from Dante's *Inferno*.

Raphael both worked in Rome for more than ten years, for the same popes, in the same Vatican palaces, with the same intention of employing art to give visible form to the same religious credo, at the time threatened by the serious crisis of the Roman church. Raphael believed God was revealed in the providential order of nature and history; centuries of human error had obscured and distorted the revelation. Art, in its quest for beauty, would eliminate the distracting contradictions and restore clarity with form and proportion, reflecting the order of the creative intellect. Beauty was, in fact, quite simply the result of those harmonious proportions, the revelation of them; beauty was an extra to the truth of dogma as it was also a sign of God's desire to abandon mystery and communicate directly with man in order to bring about his salvation. For Michelangelo history and nature too were familiar and recognizable realities, and had therefore to be overcome in order to achieve a rapport with God unaffected and uninhibited by the senses. It was, in a way, a private revelation to an artist chosen to then communicate it to the world. Those forms and words therefore did not only communicate, but they actually made the divine desire for revelation a reality. Thus they had to be familiar, but at the same time to change, visibly transforming and surpassing their natural limits.

Raphael, the *School of Athens* (1509-1510), detail. Rome, Vatican Palace, Stanza della Segnatura.

**Restoration
of the *Doni Madonna*
and the vault
of the Sistine Chapel
revealed more
fully the importance
Michelangelo's
painting had for early
Tuscan mannerism.
The dissonant
colours and the
violence
of movement
in Rosso Fiorentino's
painting derive
from Michelangelo's
work and from the
destroyed cartoon for
the *Battle of Cascina*.**

Consequently they were in a state of tension which rarely evolved into a conclusive action. The supreme example of the attempt to reconcile word and expression is the ceiling of the Sistine chapel; here painting transforms visual spectacle into sensitive vision, the virtual revelation present in the universal nature of the divine. The Prophets and the Sibyls have, of necessity, human bodies and faces though their expressions and movements reveal their internal and divine dynamism; however, it is their name, boldly written across the plinth of their thrones, which makes, or rather 'nominates', them Prophets and Sibyls, chosen to receive and communicate the Word. In addition to the explicit relationship, the deeply intense colours, now revealed once more by restoration, demonstrate that Michelangelo did not consider nature to be the source and inspiration for his kind of 'beauty': the colours were suggestive of the divine precisely because they were not 'natural' and they were at one and the same time transformations and visualizations of the supernatural, without becoming natural.

Above:
The *Doni Madonna*
(1506-1507).
Florence,
Galleria degli Uffizi.

Right:
Rosso Fiorentino,
*Moses
and the Daughters
of Jethro*
(1523).
Florence
Galleria degli Uffizi.

The dialectic of opposites

NOT ONLY THE visible forms of painting and sculpture, but words too assumed a revelatory sense when placed in contexts different to the syntactical-rhetorical order of Ciceronian discourse. In fact, poetry had a construction which dislocated words in such a way that, freed from any logical-discursive relationships, their meaning was enhanced. Binni rightly clarified the relationship between the poems written with the clear intention of making poetry and the letters, written without any attempt to create literary prose.

The letters, mainly written for practical reasons concerning his family and work, demonstrate, perhaps not surprisingly, an unusual existentialist intensity. All manner of daily event, no matter how big or small, became a profound existentialist problem in the mind of the artist, reminding him of the anguished problem of existence which could only be resolved by religion.

The letters demonstrate the quite unusual quality of the verbal content of the poetry; but this quality is achieved by the transformation of normal constructions, and the framing of a new context which highlights the 'intrinsic value' of the words. Indeed, the incisive structural analysis of Gambon focused on the originality of the poetic structure. Compared to the syntactical logic of Cicero's rhetoric, it represented a new process of symbolization, passing from the unconscious to the transcendental, avoiding the intermediate stage of logical discourse. For Gambon, this was the reason why Michelangelo's poetry, although underrated by the critics, so greatly impressed modern poets such as Montale and Ungaretti. Just as life leaves its mark, so the poems quite often reflect Michelangelo's ideas on art, beauty and the bitter struggle and frequent disappointments inherent in the work of an artist. Three famous lines synthesize his philosophy:

> *"The best of artists hath no thought to show*
> *Which the rough stone in its superfluous shell*
> *Doth not include..."* *.

The theme of the pre-existence of the idea is Neoplatonic and was already present in Alberti's treatise on painting, the reference to which is obvious when Michelangelo calls "circoscrizione" the outline of a drawing.

The notion is repeated in a madrigal to Vittoria Colonna:

Left:
Rebellious Slave (1513). Paris, Musée du Louvre. **Symbolizing the struggle of the mind against the chains of the flesh, the prisoner writhes, restrained by the material, in the non-finito of the rough stone.**

* *"Non ha l'ottimo artista alcun concetto / ch'un marmo solo in se non circoscriva / col suo superchio..."*

Above:
Decorative detail on the shorter side of the tombs, Florence, San Lorenzo, New Sacristy (1520-1537). **In contrast to the non-finito is the extreme attention to decorative elements - two aspects of Michelangelo's mannerist style.**

Opposite page:
Giuliano de' Medici,
duke of Nemours
(1526-1534).
Florence,
San Lorenzo,
New Sacristy.

> *"Just as we put, O Lady, by subtraction,*
> *Into the rough, hard stone*
> *A living figure, grown*
> *Largest wherever rock has grown most small…"* *.

The insistence on the technical act of 'subtraction' which assumes the character of a spiritual act, of sublimation, is typical of Michelangelo. The removal of the material was not simply a matter of chiselling away the mass of stone. The process was the same for poetry:

> *"Just as in pen and ink*
> *Are elevated, plain and middle styles,*
> *In marble noble or lowly forms*
> *According to the mind that draws them forth…"* **.

The comparison of sculpture and writing could hardly be more explicit, yet why write of pen and ink instead of the blank page, unless the reference is to a quality generated by the hand and the tools it uses? The first two lines could even refer to drawing, a form of writing with pen and ink: thus it is drawing which links art and poetry, almost physically. Their relationship formed a mechanism which had a precise, although not a primary, function in the mental dynamics of the artist.

Michelangelo continually queried and analysed: where did the sensory limits of art lie, to what extent must the visual perception of the physical intensify its rhythm, accelerate its pressure, in order to finally aspire to the sublime?

In order to understand the role that poetry played in the evolution of Michelangelo's artistic theory, we must remember that while the goal was transcendent purity, the origins lay with Donatello, Brunelleschi, Masaccio and the great theoretical cornerstone of Humanist art - Alberti's treatise.

Alberti quite clearly stated that the painter is not interested in the 'non-visible': "the painter's only study is to copy what he sees". Michelangelo only represented things which were non-visible, or were made visible only by the light of revelation, and this was precisely why their 'visibility' had to be intensified and reinforced. Like Petrarch he thought of beauty which passes from the eyes into the heart and he fully appreciated the importance of visual impact: "my eyes are enchanted by beautiful things"; "my eyes are greedy for wonders of all kinds"; "my body might be only an eye", and so on. Sensory perception was an obstacle to be overcome, and the more intense the experience, the more the spirit was elevated. In the same way sensual love was sinful, but without it the love of God would not have existed: Eros had two faces, but was one.

In the *Last Judgement* the gigantic form of the bodies signifies, by contradiction, that they transcend their physical nature. The sincere or (like Aretino) hypocritical devotees of the Counter-Reformation were not, after all, entirely mistaken, for though the nudes may not have been indecent as they claimed, they did, however, proudly celebrate the restitution of the flesh at the hour of the final judgement.

When Michelangelo affirmed that artists should have compasses in their eyes, he certainly did not intend to suggest that banal empiricism should replace the mathematical theories of proportion; he understood that seeing was in itself an ontological act. To see was also to name, however: the linear outline of the figures had a finite sense, it contained the image as the word contained the concept. Here too, obviously, there was a contradiction between finite and infinite, and the same contradiction was present in the 'non-finito' which expressed more than the

* *"Sì come per levar, donna, si pone / in pietra alpestre e dura / una viva figura, / che là più cresce u' più la pietra scema….."*
** *"Sì come nella penna e nell'inchiostro / è l'alto e 'l basso e 'l mediocre stile, / e ne' marmi l'immagin ricca o vile, / secondo che 'l sa trar l'ingegno nostro…."*

Michelangelo
was often criticised
for the lack of any
similarity between
the dukes
and the statues
on their tombs.
He replied,
«No one will remember what they looked
like a thousand years
from now».
He clearly disliked
purely imitative art.
In the case
of the Medici tombs,
the statues
of the deceased were
not intended
to be portraits:
the dukes had
to represent moral
and ideal values.

*The Resurrection
of Christ,*
(1532).
London, British
Museum.

'finito' and was therefore the true 'finito'.

The principle of contradiction was at the basis of Neoplatonism and Michelangelo's philosophy and the intense dynamism of his figures is created by precisely that oscillation between opposing forces. It is quite understandable that his contemporaries considered him to be an absolute master of the technique of foreshortening which does indeed require compasses in the eyes: it was the dialectic method of making the furthest point of an image contiguous to the nearest, or of covering the longest distance with the shortest route, which is the same thing.

The conceptual and verbal structure of the *Rime* is founded entirely on contradiction, as if each concept (and each image was fixed in a concept) could only be defined as being the antithesis of its opposite. The frequency of opposing concepts in Michelangelo's poetry is, without doubt, one of the most obvious features of his manneristic extremism.

To quote just some such examples: "All others for pleasure, yet I for pain", "it burns me, but in burning freezes still", "I will be as ice in fire", "I live of my death", "I live happy in my unhappy fate", "who kills me, protects me", "it serves me most where

**The drawing
may be part of
a preliminary design
for the decoration
of the New Sacristy,
referring to
the frescoed scene
of the Resurrection
of Christ which
was to have been
painted above
the far tomb.**

there is greatest pain", "I am early and late", "from gentle weeping to a painful smile", "from an eternal to a brief peace", "cold in the sun, hot in the chill of mists", "forgiving of others and only with himself severe", "love and cruelty are my life's battlefield: the one is armed of compassion, the other, death; the one kills me the other keeps me alive" and so on.

There is obviously an analogy with drawing, where foreshortening is not a technique of perspective, but a stylistic principle whereby a single sign defines distance and proximity on the same surface. In drawing as in poetry, however, the oscillating movement from high to low is associated with the marked tendency to formulate concepts, each concept being defined in relation to its opposite. For Michelangelo concept and image were the same thing, they had the same density and the same finality, and this identity extended to the word which had to be defined by its own phonetic and syllabic structure, as the image was defined by its linear outline. In the debate concerning language those who supported Florentine vernacular emphasized the precision and conceptual density of Tuscan speech. Towards the end of the century, the Accademia della Crusca began work on the first 'dictionary' of the Italian language; as the purpose of the work was to provide definitions, it clearly had to conceptualize every word.

Already earlier in the century, however, the need to conceptualize nomenclature had been part of Machiavelli's political reasoning. In the *Decennali* which related recent history in poetic form, all virtues, vices and aspects of character were seen as concepts and were characterized by a capital letter, such as Fortune, Fraud, Envy, Repentance, Avarice, Sloth, Need. Indeed, so rigorous was Machiavelli concerning the Florentine language, that he wished even to distinguish it from Tuscan.

Within the poetical texts, the crystalline sharpness of the word-concept is even more striking due to its isolation and finality, its freedom from the logic of discourse implicit within grammatical and syntactical relationships. Consequently the construction of poetry was quite different to the construction of prose. This is most clearly seen in the vain attempts of critics and commentators to transform the more abstruse and complex passages into prose hoping thus to render them less obscure.

The result has always been so disappointing that one can only agree with Croce's severely critical opinion of the general futility and pointless difficulty of the conceptual content. Why then did a contemporary such as Berni, who detested Petrarch's courtly style, so praise Michelangelo for writing ideas instead of words? What exactly was he saying in his poetic writings? It is true that only rarely did the conceptual content have any real concrete substance; it was rather a transcription of the intense, existentialist rhythm of a restless and anxious mind which used poetry as a means of symbolization, perhaps artificially tortuous but, in the end, liberating. The liberation was even greater as, not having literary roots, it did not require that professional expertise which to Michelangelo the painter and sculptor was unique.

That rare essence of the word was to be found in the firmness of the outline, in the tonal strength, the jewel-like glint which single words acquire, precisely when they lack harmonious association, in that abnormal context which does not follow the logic of discourse but dislocates the verbal elements according to the pulsating beat of a supreme and turbulent mind which saw everything in terms of either destructive or stimulating contradiction.

The words, which did of course have an everyday sense, were, in the poetic context, like the faces, bodies and clothes of the Prophets and Sibyls – nothing more than screens to intercept

Victory
(c. 1532-1534).
Florence,
Palazzo Vecchio,
Salone
dei Cinquecento.

**The much debated
significance
of the sculpture
is, in fact, evident
in the general
characteristics
and the gesture
of the youth
who represses
the old man.
In Michelangelo
the spiralling
movement
and the twisting
line assume
the quality
of a concept
which encapsulates
the idea.**

Opposite page:
Head of a goddess
(or *Cleopatra*)
(1533-1534).
Florence,
Casa Buonarroti.

and communicate messages which otherwise could not be grasped. Moreover, the language was on the whole similar to that in current use – a difficulty to be overcome. In the manneristic poetics which Michelangelo himself helped to create, all art was the result of overcoming difficulties, whether real or imaginary.

Difficulty meant contradiction and contrast such as, in the *Rime*, love and death, hope and disappointment, virtue and sin, humility and vanity. It was not the content of the concepts which mattered, but the dynamics of their contradictions: to look for meaning in their continual convolutions is like demanding that the nude figures moving and gesturing on the ceiling of the Sistine chapel should explain why they are so restless and where they want to go.

Those exaggerated and unprovoked movements are simply the release of an energy until now repressed: symmetry, proportional order, the harmony of natural elements and historic events is daringly contradicted. There is a contrast between objective, classical beauty (as portrayed by Raphael) and subjective beauty:

> *"Tell me, Love, I beseech thee, if my eyes*
> *truly see the beauty which is the breath of my being,*
> *or if it is only an inward image I behold when,*
> *wherever I look,*
> *I see the carven image of her face..." **

Thus beauty is not the external cause of love - it is instead love itself which formulates its own object. As love is a state of being for the subject, it does not change according to the, in any case casual, fact that its object is a man or a woman, a real person such as Tommaso Cavalieri or Vittoria Colonna, or a product of the imagination such as the beauteous and cruel woman.

Below:
The three tasks
of Hercules
(1530-1533).
Windsor Library.

Michelangelo mingles the platonic theme of beauty with a bizarre and fantastic style; Piero di Cosimo provided an iconographic precedent with a work entitled *Simonetta Vespucci* .

* *"Dimmi di grazia, Amor, se gli occhi miei / veggono 'l ver della beltà c'aspiro / o s'io l'ho dentro allor che, dov'i' miro, / veggio scolpito el viso di costei...".*

Historical criticism of Michelangelo's poetry

Letter written
by Michelangelo
(1511-1512),
with a sketch
by the artist showing
himself painting
the ceiling
of the Sistine Chapel.
Florence,
Casa Buonarroti.

"Ho visto qualche sua composizione: / sono ignorante, e pur direi d'avelle / lette tutte nel mezzo di Platone".

As a poet Michelangelo was certainly no amateur – it was simply not in his nature. A reading of his sonnets, madrigals, verses, and songs is neither easy nor even enjoyable – the struggle to compose as well as the tenacious quest for perfection can both be felt. The fact that they were set to music by rather mediocre musicians of the day does not mean that they were, even superficially, harmonious, the fame of the author was enough to ensure their success. While still alive, the manuscripts were read by a limited group of scholars: Francesco Berni, Benedetto Varchi, Donato Giannotti and, of course, Tommaso Cavalieri and Vittoria Colonna to whom many compositions were dedicated. One of these literary gentlemen, Luigi del Riccio, planned to publish a selection of the verses and Michelangelo, always mindful of his fame as an artist, agreed and collaborated. Riccio died in 1546, however, and the plan came to nothing. Michelangelo continued writing poetry for the rest of his life without considering publication. The later poems, in fact, are quite beyond literary analysis: they reflect the religious torment which, after completing the Pauline Chapel, lead him to abandon painting and to an increasing 'dematerialization' in his rare sculptural forms.

Even though it is obvious that the supreme beauty and skill of Michelangelo's figurative and architectural work overshadowed his poetical writings, they were not widely known until the last century. After the *Last Judgement* the narrow-minded supporters of the Counter-Reformation clearly viewed his transcendental religiosity with great suspicion. Consequently his poetry was neglected until 1623, when his nephew, Michelangelo the younger, decided to publish it. Unfortunately though, he altered the original text to make it more legible and, even worse, he removed the passages where the homosexual eroticism of his famous relative was clearly evident. It was still preferable not to mention this tendency, or his religious apprehensions, despite the fact both were acceptable within the terms of Michelangelo's Neoplatonism.

The first of Michelangelo's contemporaries to understand that his poetry was not to be confused with the fashionable courtliness of Petrarch was, without doubt, Berni – generally better renowned for his satire than his compliments. He referred to him as "Apollo-Apelles" and while it may only have been an amusing play on words, it summed up with perfect insight the conceptual content of the poems compared to the facile nature of the elegantly fashionable Petrarch: "he speaks of ideas while you have only words"; and his ideas were concepts clearly derived from Platonism:

> *"I have seen some of his compositions:*
> *I am ignorant, yet I could swear that*
> *I had read them somewhere in Plato"* *.

After almost two centuries of neglect, which even the 1623 edition did nothing to improve, the romantic poets discovered in Michelangelo the figure of the inspired genius. Ugo Foscolo was the first to discover the importance of

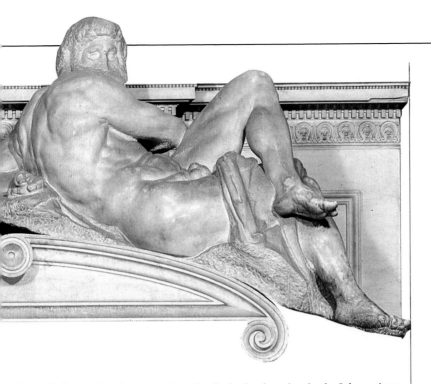

Tomb of Giuliano de' Medici with the figures of *Day* and *Night* (1526-1531). Florence, San Lorenzo, New Sacristy.

The *Medici Madonna* (1521-1534) Florence, San Lorenzo, New Sacristy.

his poetic legacy, but in comparing the 'imitative imagination' of the artist to the 'creative imagination' of the poet, which he considered to be less powerful, the work was undervalued. The fundamental error of making comparisons instead of looking for relationships, continued until the time of Benedetto Croce – the creator of the poems was, after all, the great Michelangelo who was more of a poet in painting and sculpture than in poetry. As a poet he was merely an amateur and, since he could not even claim to be a man of letters, a mediocre amateur, full of "inaccurate usage, expletives, obscurities, stiffness, contortions, which are quite unacceptable as they are most unpleasant".

Despite the dismissive opinions and belittling comparisons, a better consideration of Michelangelo's poetic works finally became possible when a new enlarged edition by Cesare Guasti appeared in 1863, based at last on the original writings and not on the 17th-century edition. This was followed in 1897 by the German edition of Karl Frey, whose dating was rather debatable. After numerous other editions, all more or less complete and based on Guasti but prefaced by various illustrious names (Giovanni Amendola, Giovanni Papini, Valentino Piccoli), the definitive critical edition by Enzo Noè Girardi was published in 1960 by Laterza in the series 'Scrittori d'Italia'.

Revision of the accepted critical opinion began in 1941 with a work by Valerio Mariani, still comparative, but positively so. Mariani considered that the poetry reflected the innermost beliefs of the artist and could be interpreted as a sort of 'interior biography' describing the daily torments caused by art rather than by everyday life. In fact, the relationship with art was bound to exist, but it was, by analogy, inspirational. The questions of the poetry's genuine autonomy and the right relationship between it and figurative art were analytically resolved in studies by Robert J. Clements (1966), Walter Binni (1975) and Glauco Gambon (1985).

Clements still insisted on the parallel between literary and figurative poetics, both based on Neoplatonic concepts which dated from Michelangelo's youth, when he was influenced by the Medici cultural circle, including Poliziano and Marsilio Ficino. The definition of 'Michelangelo, Baroque poet' is at first surprizing, though it has nothing to do with the old, now refuted, concept of 'Michelangelo, father of the Baroque'. Clements referred to the ascetic-mystical element present in 17th-century poetry of Neoplatonic inspiration, from Gongora to Donne, and including Shakespeare's sonnets which, without doubt, have some quite striking similarities to Michelangelo's poetry that none of the 17th-century poets, on the whole more mannerist than Baroque, could have recognized.

It was Gambon, however, who pointed out the strongly mannerist character of the poetry in his perceptive structural analysis of not only the linguistic, syntactical and metrical aspects, but also of what could be referred to as the conceptual iconology of Michelangelo's poems. In fact, the use of an accepted language and the classical poetic forms constituted a set of rules, the wilful or capricious transgression of which represented an intense and forceful expressive desire.

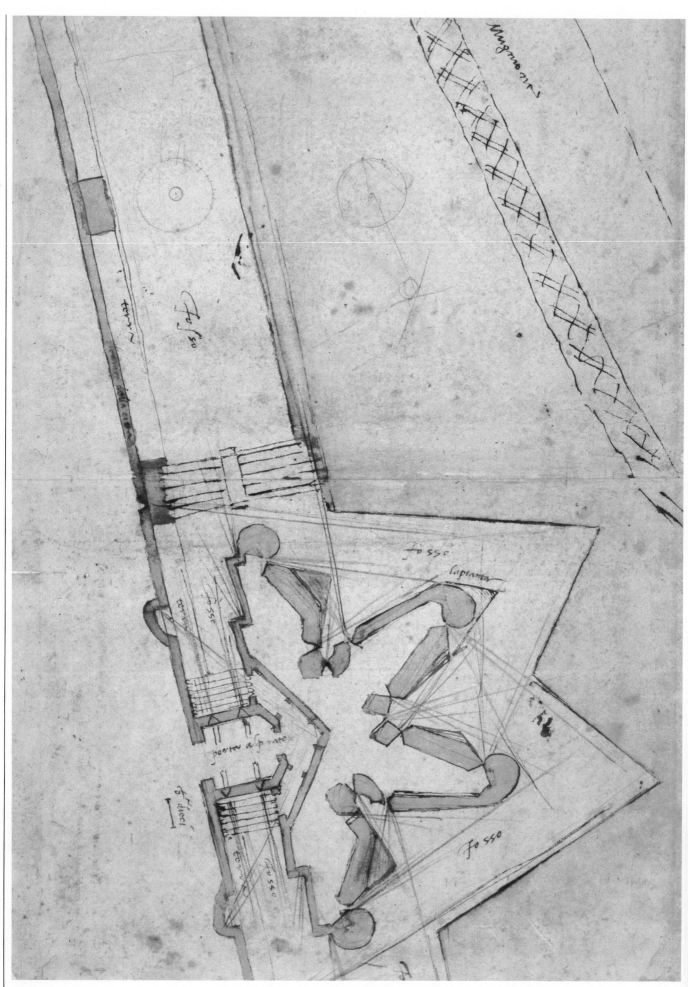

Breaking
the rules

ichelangelo's Neoplatonism, which with the passing of time moved increasingly from an intellectual to a religious plane, sought to achieve not simply a substantial unity of the arts as in drawing, but much more a profound and indissoluble unity of art, existence and salvation. To achieve this unity it was necessary to transcend the concept of art as imitation, the emulation of an external reality, whether in nature or the antique, used simply as a model. This was the essential problem of art and all others stemmed from it. The more the experience of transcending the sensory element or the historic model was difficult and virtuous, the more vivid and intense it was:

> *"As the flame more teased by the wind grows stronger,*
> *the more are the virtues loved by heaven*
> *abused, the more they shine..."* *.

In the figurative arts the ascent could not be direct; one gained an impression of the divine only by seeing it reflected in a physical form. In poetry instead, as soon as the physical nature of an object was defined with a name, it was no longer relevant and everything depended on the location of the word in the poetic context. Thus in the *Rime* there are always key words, the poetic sense of which depended on their anomalous position compared to that in a logical-syntactical discourse. Such as, for example:

> *"All anger, all misery and all violence,*
> *he who is armed with Love conquers all fortune"* **.

The most fundamental problems in art were not, however, the objects which were imitated, whether natural or classical, but the fact of imitation itself, at one and the same time an act of possession and servitude. The contradiction appears even more absurd since obedience and liberating deviation occurred simultaneously. Except, of course in religion as was the case with Michelangelo who at the time of his 'conversion' reflected at length on the *Imitatio Christi*, – the imitation of that which could not be imitated. It was also a fundamental factor in the religious debate which took place in Florence with Savonarola and culminated in the rebellion of Luther who believed a more severe servitude would lead to a more glorious liberation.

Left:
design for the
fortifications
of Florence
(1527).
Florence,
Casa Buonarroti.

Saint Matthew
(1505-1506).
Florence,
Galleria
dell'Accademia.

* *"Come fiamma più cresce più contesa / dal vento, ogni virtù ch'l cielo esalta / tanto più splende quant'è più offesa..."*

** *"Ogn'ira, ogni miseria e ogni forza, / chi d'Amor s'arma vince ogni fortuna"*

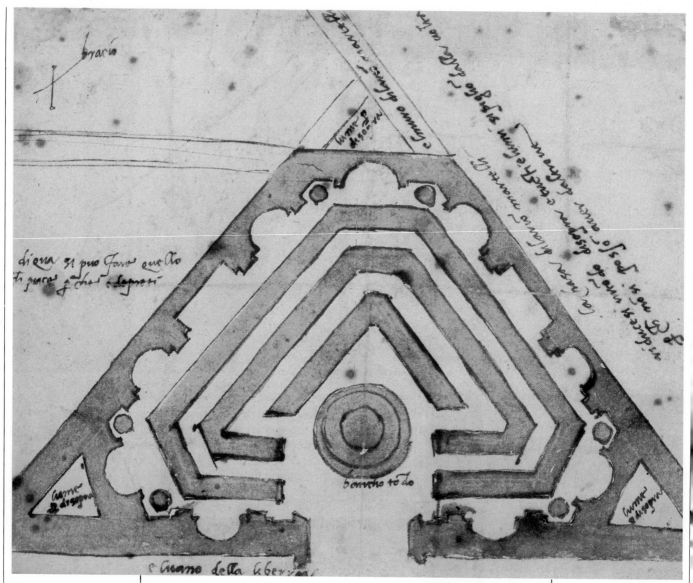

Plan
for the *Small Study*
in the Laurentian
Library
(before 1525).
Florence,
Casa Buonarroti.
**With Michelangelo
architecture becomes
a series of highly
modulated volumes,
at times
not dissimilar
to organic forms.**

It is not true that architecture was by its very nature a non-imitative art – to praise a structure one did not say it was built, but that it was born. It was not imitation to observe the laws of static equilibrium in the construction and to represent them within the physical form, but a way of obliging the artist to respect natural forces. If imitation of classical architecture was difficult because the surviving documents, such as Vitruvius' treatise, did not provide a general rule, they did, however, provide a vocabulary, an institutionalized morphology. The forms of the columns, the capitals, bases, mouldings all represented a code which it was difficult to ignore. It seemed impossible to formulate an architectural 'vernacular', the art of architecture being too closely bound to the most solid and enduring institutions. Yet Michelangelo's great achievement, albeit foreseen by Brunelleschi and Giuliano da Sangallo (much less so by Alberti), was in fact the creation of an illustrious, even transcendental, vernacular architecture. It is evident in the extraordinary designs for the Florentine fortifications which, without making the slightest reference to accepted rules, completely revolutionized traditional defensive building and, by not making any allowances for the countryside invaded nature with incredible violence. Nor were these inventive exceptions perhaps stimulated by patriotic fervour: the 'fearsome' structural deviation seen in the ramparts is perfectly in keeping with the vestibule of the Biblioteca Laurenziana, the piazza and staircase of the Campidoglio and the articulated masses of Saint Peter's

Michelangelo devoted himself almost entirely to architecture after the 'conversion' which demanded that his relationship with God should be direct and not mediated or filtered by either nature or history: the relationship was no longer seen in terms of life but of death. The abjuration of figurative art was explicit:

> *"What is the sense of making all those chubby babies*
> *if it brings me to the same end as he*
> *who crossed the sea and then drowned in snot?*
> *Great art, where for a while I was well considered,*
> *has brought me to this,*
> *poor, old and forced to serve others,*
> *ruined if I don't soon die"* *.

It is the most despondent of confessions. Figurative art which had brought him so much success no longer had meaning for him. Nor did he consider architecture, to which he now devoted himself almost exclusively, to be an art but a service or duty, a belief which is evident in many of his letters. Poetry, like architecture, had its rules: the various classical formations of the single elements, the rhymes, the symbolic rigidity of the vocabulary. Although obliged to make use of that vocabulary one could however transform, if not the literal meaning of the words, their expressive power within a certain context. In architecture refusal to adhere to the traditional rules of proportion fragments the descriptive elements, separates

The Vestibule (1559). Florence, Biblioteca Laurenziana. **The stairway was built by Bartolomeo Amannati based on a terrecotta model made by Michelangelo.**

* *"Che giova voler fare tanti bambocci, / se mi ha condotto al fin, come colui / che passò 'l mar e poi affogò ne' mocci? / L'arte pregiata, ov'alcun tempo fui / di tanta opinion, mi rec'a questo, / povero, vecchio e servo in forz'altrui / ch'io son disfatto, s'i'non muoio presto".

them from the logic of static equilibrium, isolates and intensifies them; they are forced to restitute the energy which they should have developed, neutralized and transmitted to the sculptural power of the form. It is a continual conflict between acceptance and transgression: this is also why the mannerist philosophy can be more clearly seen in architecture and poetry than in sculpture and painting. The means of expression were still clearly those of classicism - no others existed; but the entirely Florentine terseness of their use and interpretation, their detachment, even in terms of colour, the anomalous spaces, are all clear signs of a sort of formal euphemism which is exactly the opposite of Michelangelo's legendary, though unmerited, fame for the colossal.

He was never, however, a builder in the traditional sense of the word: as Ackerman pointed out, he always worked on existing structures, though his architecture is no less inventive for that. Moreover, it was a constant theme in all his work: to create from nothing would still have meant imitating the processes of nature, while he instead radically transformed or overturned the existing meaning of things. At the end of his life, with a few inspired touches, he turned the pagan tepidarium of Diocletian's baths into the Christian church of Santa Maria degli Angeli, from the 'idolum' he made the 'templum Virginis'. It was the final synthesis of his aspirations: he succeeded in preserving almost entirely a classical context while changing its meaning. In his old age the cupola of San Pietro tormented him, but it was not the obviously difficult problem of its construction which worried him, rather the line of the curve. It had to harmonize two opposites, the defined volume of the spherical vault and the infinite space of the heavens which had to be both natural and empyrean. He did not hide his intention of repeating Brunelleschi's miracle, but he transformed its meaning from Tuscan to universal.

Vasari realised that in the Medici chapel of San Lorenzo Michelangelo was most interested in the 'ornamentation' which imposed its intense rhythm onto the proportions of Brunelleschi's structure and altered the original form to such an extent that it seemed to dissolve the physical enclosure and establish a relationship of contrast between the empty perspective of the niches and the invasive mass of the tombs. Vasari himself felt that the intensity of the decoration, either too close or too distant in traditional terms, was quite marvellous, but should not be imitated. The rhythm of this alternately leisurely and impulsive pace is, however, structurally similar to that of poetry – a frequently contradictory rhythm which surpasses itself to reach a higher, more subtle and quintessential arrhythmia. Lexical elements, both architectural and literary, when detached from an intentionally disharmonious syntax, acquired a prominence which establishes them as existing in their own right, free of any descriptive relationship.

The novel character of Michelangelo's architecture was the same as that of his poetry. It is no mere coincidence that his poetic activity was most consistent and incisive during the period in Florence when he worked on the sacristy and library of San Lorenzo. The vestibule of the latter, which in terms of its construction is full of inconsistencies is, without doubt, the most 'poetic' of his architectural works and perhaps also, together with the unhappy final version of Julius II's tomb in San Pietro in Vincoli in Rome, is the most explicitly and uninhibitedly manneristic.

Michelangelo violently but coherently objected to the classical relationship between construction-noun and decoration-adjective. Once that relationship were broken, the decoration, now the principle feature rather than mere accessory, subjugated the logic of constructional statics to its own purely idealistic energy. In overcoming the pre-existing limitation one was, at last, liberated from it.

CHRONOLOGY

1483 — Raphael is born in Urbino. Leonardo signs the contract for the *Virgin of the Rocks.*

1485 — Probable year of birth of Titian.

1486 — Ghirlandaio and his workshop begin decorating the chancel of Santa Maria Novella (completed 1490).

1488 — Andrea Verrocchio, florentine sculptor, dies in Venice. | Comes to Florence as an apprentice in Ghirlandaio's workshop. Despite Michelangelo's later denials, various contemporaries confirmed this fact. Of the three years apprenticeship, he has served one.

1492 — Lorenzo de' Medici dies. Alexander VI (of the Borgia family) is elected pope. Christopher Columbus discovers America. Piero della Francesca dies. | His earliest works date from this period: the *Battle of Hercules with the Centaurs*, the wooden *Crucifix* for Santo Spirito, and the *Madonna of the Steps.*

1494 — Charles VIII, king of France, invades the Italian peninsula. Piero de' Medici is driven out of Florence and the Republic is proclaimed. Savonarola's preachings gain force. | Flees to Venice before Charles VIII enters Florence. He later moves to Bologna where he makes an *Angel* candelabrum for the sarcophagus of Saint Dominic.

1495 — Leonardo begins the *Last Supper.* In Florence Perugino opens a flourishing workshop. | Returns to Florence where he makes small sculptures for Lorenzo di Pierfrancesco de' Medici.

1496 — In June he visits Rome as a guest of cardinal Raffaele Riario. He makes a *Cupid* (lost) and a figure of *Bacchus* (Florence, Bargello).

1498 — Under pressure from Alexander VI, Savonarola is tried and burnt at the stake. Antonio Pollaiolo dies in Rome. | On 27 August he signs a contract with the French cardinal Jean Bilhères to make the *Pietà.* The work is to be completed within a year and the price agreed is 450 ducats.

1499 — Luca Signorelli begins the frescoes in the San Brizio chapel, Orvieto cathedral. | The client for the *Pietà* dies on 6 August.

1500 — Louis XII invades the Italian peninsula. The Sforza are driven out of Milan. Leonardo returns to Florence. Bramante is working in Rome. Botticelli paints the *Mystic Nativity.* | Contract for an altar panel in the church of Sant'Agostino, Rome. The work may be the *Burial of Christ* in the National Gallery, London, although the attribution is uncertain.

1501 — Raphael produces his first works at Città di Castello. | Returns to Florence. On 5 June he is commissioned to make some sculptures for the Piccolomini altar in Siena Cathedral. On 16 August the Florentine republic commissions him to make the *David.*

1502 — Pier Soderini is made *Gonfaloniere* of the Florentine Republic for life. | On 12 August the Republic commissions a second *David* from him for the cardinal Pierre de Rohan. The work is later completed by Benedetto da Rovezzano.

1503 — Alexander VI dies suddenly. After the brief papacy of Pius III, Julius II (Rovere family), an opponent of Alexander's political policy, is elected pope. Collapse of the state of Cesare Borgia, son of Alexander VI. Leonardo begins the battle of Anghiari. | On 24 April the Opera del Duomo commission 12 statues of Apostles from him for the cathedral interior. Only *Saint Matthew* is roughed out. On 14 December the Flemish cloth merchant, Alexandre Moscrou, pays him 50 ducats for the *Bruges Madonna.*

1475 — Michelangelo Buonarroti is born at Caprese on 6 March, second son of the magistrate, Lodovico di Leonardo.

1478 — The Pazzi Conspiracy, instigated by pope Sixtus IV, fails; Giuliano de' Medici is killed in the fray, but the authority of his brother, Lorenzo, is consolidated as a result.

1481 — Sandro Botticelli probably begins painting both the *Primavera* and the *Birth of Venus* in this year. Leonardo begins the *Adoration of the Magi.* | His mother dies. First lessons at the grammar school. Meets the painter Francesco Granacci who encourages him to draw.

1482 — The paintings in the Sistine Chapel in the Vatican, where Perugino and Botticelli were the foremost artists, are completed.

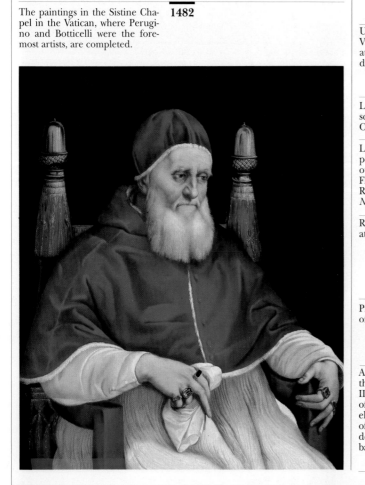

HISTORICAL AND ARTISTIC EVENTS		LIFE OF MICHELANGELO
Raphael moves to Florence. With the Treaty of Blois, the Kingdom of Naples falls under Spanish rule.	1504	Commissioned to fresco the *Battle of Cascina*. On 8 September the *David* is brought to Piazza della Signoria. In October he receives a second payment from the merchant Alexandre Moscrou.
Bramante begins work on the Little temple of San Pietro in Montorio and the Cortile del Belvedere.	1505	In March Pope Julius II commissions him to make his tomb. Michelangelo goes to Carrara until the end of the year to choose the marble.
Julius II defeats Bologna. The *Laocoön* is discovered in Rome. Bramante begins to build the new church of Saint Peter. Leonardo departs for Milan.	1506	He returns to Rome, but unable to obtain confirmation for Julius' tomb he leaves the city and returns to Florence. In Bologna on 21 November he is reconciled with the pope who requests him to make a bronze statue of himself.
Raphael paints the Baglioni *Deposition*	1507	Probably the year in which the *Doni Madonna* was painted.
The League of Cambrai: Julius II, Maximilian of Hapsburg, Louis XII and Ferdinand the Catholic join forces against Venice. Alonso Berruguete is in Florence.	1508	The monument to Julius II is inaugurated in Bologna on 21 February. Michelangelo returns to Florence where the *Gonfaloniere* Pier Soderini commissions him to make a statue of *Hercules and Cacus*. Returns to Rome in April. On 10 May he accepts the task of frescoing the ceiling of the Sistine chapel.
Venice is defeated at Agnadello. Baldassarre Peruzzi designs the Villa Farnesina for Agostino Chigi. In Rome Raphael begins work on the *Stanze*.	1509	
The Holy League of Julius II, Ferdinand the Catholic, and Venice is formed against France. Sebastiano del Piombo arrives in Rome. Andrea del Sarto begins the scenes from the *Life of the Virgin* in the Cloister of SS Annunziata.	1511	On 14 or 15 August Julius II visits the Sistine chapel, which is as yet unfinished.
The Medici return to Florence. In Siena Beccafumi paints the *Trinity Triptych*, in Florence Fra Bartolomeo paints the *Mystic Marriage of Saint Catherine*.	1512	The Sistine chapel is re-opened on 31 October. The frescoes were completed 20 days earlier.
Julius II dies. Succeeded by Giovanni de' Medici (Lorenzo il Magnifico's son) who takes the name Leo X. Leonardo is in Rome.	1513	In February a new contract for the tomb of Julius II is signed.
Bramante dies. Raphael succeeds him as chief architect of Saint Peter's; he paints the Sibyls in the Chigi chapel in Santa Maria del Pace in Rome and begins to decorate the *Stanza dell'Incendio*.	1514	Receives a commission to make the figure of the *Risen Christ* for Santa Maria sopra Minerva. The papal chapel in Castel Sant'Angelo is made to his design.
Francis I becomes king of France. With the victory of Marignano he retakes Milan. Raphael makes the cartoons for the tapestries in the Sistine chapel. Machiavelli finishes writing the *Prince*. Andrea del Sarto begins the *Scenes from the Life of John the Baptist* in the Chiostro dello Scalzo. Correggio paints his first large religious work, the *San Francesco Madonna*, now in Dresden.	1515	In April he returns to Florence where he remains until 1534.

Left:
Raphael,
Portrait of Julius II
(1512), detail,
Florence,
Galleria degli Uffizi.

Lucas Cranach,
Martin Luther
(1528), detail,
Florence,
Galleria degli Uffizi.

Following pages from left to right:
Hans Holbein,
Erasmus of Rotterdam
(1523), detail.
Paris, Musée du Louvre.

Titian, *Paul III with his nephews* (1546), detail.
Naples, Museo di Capodimonte.

HISTORICAL AND ARTISTICS EVENT		LIFE OF MICHELANGELO
Charles of Hapsburg succeeds Ferdinand the Catholic as king of Spain. Ludovico Ariosto finishes the first edition of *Orlando Furioso*. Sebastiano del Piombo works on the *Deposition* now in the Hermitage, and is commissioned to decorate the Borgherini chapel in Rome.	1516	On 8 June another contract is drawn up for the tomb of Julius II further reducing the size of the project. Leo X assigns him the contract for the façade of San Lorenzo in Florence.
Luther hammered his historic 95 theses to the church door in Wittenberg beginning the Reformation. Raphael and his workshop work on the Psyche Loggia in the Farnesina Villa and the Vatican Loggias. Leonardo goes to France. Francesco della Rovere regains the Duchy of Urbino which had been under the control of the pope's nephew, Lorenzo de' Medici.	1517	

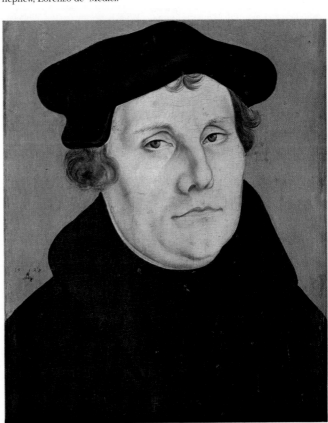

HISTORICAL AND ARTISTICS EVENT		LIFE OF MICHELANGELO
Pontormo and Rosso Fiorentino receive their first public commissions. Raphael begins the *Transfiguration* in competition with the *Resurrection of Lazarus* by Sebastiano del Piombo painted with the advice of Michelangelo.	**1518**	
Charles V of Hapsburg elected emperor of the Holy Roman Empire. Leonardo dies at Amboise. In Parma Correggio paints the *Camera della Badessa* in Saint Paul's Convent, and the following year the dome of Saint John the Evangelist.	**1519**	Leo X commissions him to design the New Sacristy in San Lorenzo, destined to house six Medici tombs.
Raphael dies unexpectedly. Luther is excomunicated with the papal bull *Exurge Domine*.	**1520**	On 10 March Leo X abandons the plan to construct the façade of San Lorenzo. The project for the Medici tombs is reduced to two monuments.
Raphael's workshop is still the most prestigious in Rome. Giulio Romano frescos the *Sala di Costantino*, Perin del Vaga the *Sala dei Pontefici*. Rosso Fiorentino paints the *Deposition* in Volterra.	**1521**	He begins work on the Medici tombs in March. In August the *Risen Christ* is placed in Santa Maria sopra Minerva in Rome.
Leo X dies and is succeeded by Adrian of Utrecht, formerly tutor to Charles V. During his brief papacy Adrian VI imposes a policy of austerity.	**1522**	
Adrian VI dies and is succeeded by Giuliano de' Medici (cousin of Leo X), who takes the name of Clement VII. Rosso Fiorentino comes to Rome. Pontormo begins work on the *Scenes from the Passion* in the Certosa of Galluzzo near Florence.	**1523**	
Giulio Romano moves to Mantova in the service of Federico Gonzaga. In Mantova work begins on Palazzo Te. Parmigianino is in Rome.	**1524**	Work is begun on the Biblioteca Laurenziana and the statues of *Dawn* and *Dusk* for the Tomb of Lorenzo de' Medici, duke of Urbino.
Victory of the Spanish at Pavia. Francesco I is taken prisoner.	**1525**	
The League of Cognac. France, the Papal States, Florence, Venice and Milan unite against Charles V. Pontormo paints the Santa Felicita *Deposition*.	**1526**	He begins work on the tomb of Giuliano, duke of Nemours, with the sculptures of *Night* and *Day*.
The sack of Rome. Peruzzi, Rosso Fiorentino, Jacopo Sansovino, Perin del Vaga, Giovanni da Udine and Parmigianino flee from the city.	**1527**	Following the expulsion of the Medici, work on the New Sacristy in San Lorenzo is halted.
France and Spain sign the Peace of Cambrai. Francesco I renounces his claim to Italy.	**1529**	Appointed defence expert, he prepares a series of plans for the fortresses protecting Florence.
Charles V crowned emperor and king of Italy by Clement VII in Bologna. In return he promises to restore the Medici to Florence. Rosso Fiorentino moves to France and remains there until his death in 1540. Correggio paints the *Danaë*, now in the Galleria Borghese in Rome.	**1530**	He paints *Leda and the Swan* (destroyed) for the duke of Ferrara. Goes into hiding after the fall of the Republic (12 August). Pardoned by pope Clement VII he continues his work on the Laurenziana and the New Sacristy.

HISTORICAL AND ARTISTIC EVENTS		LIFE OF MICHELANGELO
Alessandro de' Medici returns to Florence after the republican interlude.	**1531**	Makes the cartoon for the *Noli mi tangere* (subsequently painted by Pontormo).
	1532	New contract for the tomb of Julius II. The plan is reduced to six statues. Meets Tommaso de' Cavalieri.
	1533	Meets pope Clement VII, who is travelling to France, at San Miniato al Tedesco. The agreement to paint the *Last Judgement* possibly dates from this meeting.
Clement VII dies and is succeeded by Alessandro Farnese who choses the name of Paul III. Ignatius of Loyola founds the Company of Jesus.	**1534**	In September, probably to plan work on the *Last Judgement*, he moves to Rome, leaving the sculptures for the New Sacristy unfinished.
Rosso Fiorentino begins the decoration of the Gallery in the Chateau de Fontainebleau.	**1535**	The contract for the *Last Judgement* is confirmed by the new pope Paul III. On 1 September he is appointed painter, sculptor and architect of the Vatican Palace.
Calvin's Geneva reform. Paul III creates a commission headed by the cardinals Carafa and Contarini to propose fundamental reforms within the church. Pietro Aretino publishes the *Ragionamenti*. Vittoria Colonna writes the *Rime*.	**1536**	On 17 November Paul III releases Michelangelo from all obligations to the heirs of Julius II, whose tomb he had undertaken to complete. He is therefore free to dedicate himself entirely to the project of the *Last Judgement*.
Salviati and Jacopino del Conte work on the Oratory of San Giovanni Decollato. Titian paints the *Venus of Urbino*.	**1538**	Designs the arrangement on the Campidoglio of the equestrian statue of *Marcus Aurelius*.

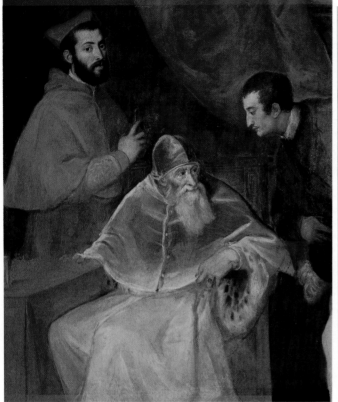

HISTORICAL AND ARTISTIC EVENTS		LIFE OF MICHELANGELO
Vittoria Colonna dies. Charles V defeats the protestant princes united in the League of Smalcalda.	**1547**	
Tintoretto paints the *Miracle of the Slave*. Ignatius of Loyola publishes the *Exercitia spiritualia*.	**1548**	
Paul III dies (December 1549) and is succeeded by Julius III. Giorgio Vasari publishes the first edition of the *Lives of the Artists*, describing artistic developments from the time of Cimabue and Giotto, ending with Michelangelo.	**1550**	Completes the frescoes in the Pauline chapel.
	1552	Completes the stairway of the Campidoglio.
	1553	Works on the *Pietà* for Florence cathedral.
Julius III dies. After the brief papacy of the reformist cardinal Marcello Cervini, Giovan Pietro Carafa is elected pope, with the name Paul IV. Charles V abdicates after the Peace of Augsburg.	**1555**	Pope Paul IV confirms his appointment as architect of Saint Peter's.
	1556	In September, with Rome under threat from the approaching Spanish army, he leaves the city intending to go to Loreto. At Spoleto he receives an instruction from the pope to return to Rome.
Elisabeth Tudor becomes Queen of England.	**1558**	
Paul IV dies and is succeeded by Pius IV, uncle of Charles Borromeo.	**1559**	Makes the designs for the church of San Giovanni dei Fiorentini and the Sforza chapel. Sends a model for the stairway of the Biblioteca Laurenziana to Florence. Probably begins the *Rondanini Pietà*.
	1560	Makes a design for the monument to Henry II of France for Catherine de' Medici. Designs the tomb of Giangiacomo dei Medici di Marignano for Milan cathedral, later made by Leone Leoni. Makes various plans for Porta Pia.
	1561	Transforms the Baths of Diocletian into the church of Santa Maria degli Angeli.
The *Accademia del Disegno* opens in Florence; Michelangelo is appointed its head, with Cosimo I de' Medici.	**1563**	
On 21 January the Congregation of the Council decides to cover up the parts of the *Universal Judgement* considered to be obscene. Daniele da Volterra is appointed to carry out the work. Tintoretto begins the decoration of the Scuola di San Rocco in Venice. Galileo Galilei is born in Pisa. Filippo Neri founds the brotherhood of the 'Oratori' in Rome. Giovanni Calvino dies on 27 May in Geneva. England restores Calais to France with the peace treaty of Troyes (11 April).	**1564**	Dies on 18 February in his house in Rome, near Trajan's Forum.

HISTORICAL AND ARTISTIC EVENTS		LIFE OF MICHELANGELO
	1539	Probably starts work on the figure of *Brutus* for cardinal Niccolò Ridolfi.
Paul III sends cardinal Pole to Viterbo: his circle includes Marcantonio Flaminio, Carnesecchi and Vittoria Colonna. Daniele da Volterra is contracted to paint the *Deposition* in the Trinità dei Monti. Michelangelo calls Perin del Vaga to work on the Sistine chapel.	**1541**	The *Last Judgement* is unveiled on 31 October. On 23 November, with the mediation of Paul III, an agreement is made with Guidobaldo della Rovere (heir of Julius II) that the tomb of the former pope may be completed by other artists, under the supervision of Michelangelo.
The Holy Office is set up in Rome. Cardinal Contarini, leader of the Catholic reform dies.	**1542**	The final contract for the tomb of Julius II is made on 20 August. Begins the frescoes in the Pauline chapel.
The decoration of Castel Sant'Angelo begins.	**1543**	
Salviati paints the *Story of Furio Camillo* in the Audience Chamber of Palazzo Vecchio.	**1543**	Designs the tomb of Francesco Bracci. The architectural structure of Julius II's tomb is completed at the end of the year in San Pietro in Vincoli.
During the Diet of Worms the "protestants" refuse to take part in the Council of Trent. Inaugural session of the Council of Trent: the beginning of the Counter-Reformation. Titian visits Rome.	**1545**	In February the statues for the tomb of Julius II are put in place. In the same month he paints a *Crucifixion* for Vittoria Colonna. Before the end of the year he completes the *Conversion of Saint Paul* in the Pauline Chapel.
Antonio da Sangallo the Younger dies. Giulio Romano dies in Mantova. Vasari paints the 100 Days Fresco in the Cancelleria.	**1546**	Appointed architect of Saint Peter's in place of Antonio da Sangallo the Younger. Commissioned to complete work on the Palazzo Farnese.

BIBLIOGRAPHY

Sources: the best editions of the biographies of Michelangelo written by Giorgio Vasari (1550 and 1568) and Ascanio Condivi (1553) are: A. Condivi, *Michelangelo. La Vita*, edited by P. D'Ancona, Milan 1928 ; G. Vasari, *La vita di Michelangelo nelle redazioni del 1550 e 1568*, edited by P. Barocchi, Milan-Naples 1962; id., *Le Vite dei più eccellenti pittori, scultori e architetti, nelle redazioni del 1550 e del 1568*, edited by R. Bettarini and P. Barocchi, Florence 1987.

Critical works and articles: J. Wilde, *Eine Studie Michelangelos nach der Antike*, in "Mitteilungen des Kunsthistorisches Institutes in Florenz", IV, 1933, pp. 41-64; K. Lanckoronscka, *Antike Elemente im Bacchus Michelangelos*, in "Dawka Sztuka", I, 1938, pp. 182-192; G. Kleiner, *Die Begegnungen Michelangelos mit der Antike*, Berlino 1950, pp. 16-18; F. Kriegbaum, *Michelangiolo und die Antike*, in "Münchner Jahrbuch der bildenden Kunst", III-IV, 1952-1953, pp. 10-36; M. Lisner, *Zu Benedetto da Maiano und Michelangelo*, in "Zeitschrift für Kunstwissenschaft", XII, 1958, pp. 141-156; id., *Il Crocifisso di Santo Spirito, Atti del convegno di studi michelangioleschi*, Roma 1964, pp. 295-316; E. Battisti, *Storia della critica su Michelangelo*, in G. Grandi, *Atti del convegno di studi michelangioleschi*, Roma 1966, pp. 177-200; id., *I coperchi delle tombe medicee*, in *Arte in Europa. Studi di storia dell'arte in onore di E. Arslan*, I, 1966, pp. 517-530; id., *The Meaning of classical Models in the Sculpture of Michelangelo*, in *Stil und Uberlieferung in der Kunst des Abendlandes*, Akten, II, Berlino 1967, pp. 73-78; C. Eisler, *"The Madonna of the Steps"*, ivi, pp. 115-121; M. Lisner, *Das Quattrocento und Michelangelo*, ivi, pp. 78-89; M. Horster, *Antike Vorstufen zum Florentiner Renaissance Bacchus*, in *Festschrift für Ulrich Middeldorf*, Berlino 1968, pp. 218-224; L. Steinberg, *Michelangelo's Florentine "Pietà": the missing Leg*, in "The Art Bulletin", 50, 1968, pp. 343-353; F. Wildt, *La Pietà Rondanini. Genesi e tecnica*, Milano 1968; M. Easton, *The Taddei Tondo: a frightened Jesus?*, in "Journal of the Warburg and Courtauld Institute", 32, 1969, pp. 391-393; S. Levine, *Tal cosa: "Michelangelo" David. Its Form, Site and political Symbolism*, New York 1969; R. W. Lightbown, *Michelangelo's great Tondo. Its Origins and Settings*, in "Apollo", 89, 1969, pp. 22-31; C. E. Gilbert, *Texts and Contexts of the Medici Chapel*, in "Art Quarterly", XXXI, 1971, pp. 391-409; H. J. Mancusi Ungaro, *Michelangelo: the Bruges Madonna and the Piccolomini Altar*, New Haven-Londra 1971; *L'opera completa di Michelangelo scultore*, a cura di U. Baldini, Milano 1973; B. Mantura, *Il primo Cristo della Pietà Rondanini*, in "Bollettino d'Arte", 58, 1973, pp. 199-201; A. Martini, *Osservazioni sul Tondo Taddei*, in "Antichità viva", 12, 1973, pp. 26-31; H. Hibbard, *Michelangelo*, Londra 1975; J. Schulz, *Michelangelo's unfinished Works*, in "The Art Bulletin", 57, 1975, pp. 366-373; F. Hartt, *Michelangelo's three Pietàs*, Londra 1977; A. Luchs, *Michelangelo's Bologna Angel: counterfeiting the Tuscan Duecento*, in "The Burlington Magazine", 120, 1978, pp. 222-225; D. Heikamp, *Scultura e politica. Le statue della Sala Grande di Palazzo Vecchio*, in *Le arti nel principato mediceo*, Firenze 1980, pp. 201-251; M. Lisner, *Form und Sinngehalt von Michelangelo's Kentaurenschlacht mit Notizen zu Bertoldo di Giovanni*, in "Mitteilungen des Kunsthistorisches Institut in Florenz", XXIV, 1980, pp. 299-344; H. Hirst, *Michelangelo in Rome: an Altarpiece and the Bacchus*, in "The Burlington Magazine", 123, 1981, pp. 580-593; E. Balas, *Michelangelo's Florentine Slaves and the S. Lorenzo's Facade*, in "The Art Bulletin", LXV, 1983, pp. 665-671; C. Carman, *Michelangelo's Bacchus and the divine Frenzy*, in "Source", 2, 1983, pp. 6-13; R. Liebert, *Michelangelo. A Psychoanalytic Study of his Life and Images*, Yale 1983; F. Verspohl, *Il David in Piazza della Signoria a Firenze, Michelangelo e Machiavelli*, in "Comunità", 37, 1983, pp. 291-356; K. Weil Garris, *On Pedestals: Michelangelo's David, Bandinelli's Hercules and Cacus, and the Sculpture of the Piazza della Signoria*, in "Römisches Jahrbuch für Kunstgeschichte", XX, 1983, pp. 377-400; J. Elkins, *Michelangelo and the human Form: his knowledge and Use of Anatomy*, in "The Art Bulletin", 7, 1984, pp. 176-186; M. Bacci, *Le fonti letterarie del Bacco di Michelangelo e il problema del committente*, in "Antichità viva", 24, 1985, pp. 131-134; M. Hirst, *Michelangelo, Carrara and the Marble for the Cardinal's Pietà*, in "The Burlington Magazine", CXXVII, 1985, pp. 154-159; C. H. Smith, *Osservazioni intorno a Il Carteggio di Michelangelo*, in "Rinascimento", XXV, 1985, pp. 4-5 e pp. 8-9; R. Ristori, *L'Aretino, il David di Michelangelo e la modestia fiorentina*, ivi, XXVII, 1986, pp. 77-97; K. Weil Garris, *Michelangelo's "Pietà" for the Cappella del Re di Francia*, in *Il se rendit in Italie. Etudes offertes à A. Chastel*, Roma-Parigi 1987, pp. 77-119; E. Balas, *Michelangelo's Victory: its Rôle and Significance*, in "Gazette des Beaux-Arts", 113, 1989, pp. 67-80; V. Shrimplin Evangelidis, *Michelangelo and Nicodemism: the Florentine Pietà*, in "The Art Bulletin", XXI, 1989, pp. 58-66; J. Larson, *The Cleaning's of Michelangelo's Taddei Tondo*, in "The Burlington Magazine", CXXXIII, 1991, pp. 844-846; G. Agosti, *Michelangelo e i Lombardi a Roma, attorno al 1500*, in "Studies in the History of Art", 33, 1992, pp. 19-36; F. Hartt, *Michelangelo in Heaven*, in "Artibus et Historiae", 13, 1992, pp. 191-200; E. Pogany Balas, *The Iconography of Michelangelo's Medici's Chapel: a new Hypothesis*, in "Gazette des Beaux-Arts", 120, 1992, pp. 171-126; W. Wallace, *Michelangelo's Roma "Pietà": Altarpiece or Grave Memorial*, in *Verrocchio and Late Quattrocento Italian Sculpture*, Firenze 1992, pp. 243-255; J. Beck, A. Paolucci, B. Santi, *Un occhio su Michelangelo*, Bergamo 1993.

Exhibition catalogues: G. Agosti, V. Farinella, *Michelangelo e l'arte classica* (Firenze, Casa Buonarroti), Firenze 1987; *The genius of the Sculptor in Michelangelo's Work* (Montreal, Museum of Fine Arts), Montreal 1992.

ACKNOWLEDGEMENTS FOR ILLUSTRATIONS

Several translations of Michelangelo's verses are taken from the following publications :
Anthony Blunt, Artistic Theory in Italy 1450-1600, *Oxford University Press, 1973.*
Michelangelo: Life, Letters and Poetry, *edited by George Bull. Oxford University Press, 1987.*

Traslation from italian by Eve Leckey

Alinari Archive, Florence: 22a, 23b, 37, 47, 49, 55b.
Giunti Archive, Florence: 4, 5, 8a, 9, 11, 13ab, 14ab, 22, 24-25, 36, 40, 44.
I.G.D.A., Milan: 1, 53, 56, 58, cover.

C. M.: 3, 34, 35, 41, 50, 52, 54b.
Massimo Listri, Florence: 39.

For back numbers of both the jurnal and the supplements:
Subscription Publication
Phone (055) 5062267
Fax (055) 5062287
Post office account 12940508 in the name of Art e Dossier, Firenze

© 1998
Giunti Gruppo Editoriale, Firenze

Direttore responsabile Bruno Piazzesi

Periodical publication Reg. Cancell. Trib. Firenze n. 3384 del 22.11.1985

Printed in Italy by Giunti Industrie Grafiche S.p.A. Prato
December 1997.

V.A.T. paid by the publischer in accordance with Article 74 lett. c - DPR 633 del 26.10.72

ISBN 88-09-76249-5